Three Political Plays

Edited by Alrene Sykes

King Richard
Steve J. Spears

The Father We Loved on a Beach by the Sea
Stephen Sewell

Irish Stew
John Bradley

University of Queensland Press

Published by University of Queensland Press, St Lucia,
Queensland, 1980
This compilation © University of Queensland Press, 1980

King Richard © Steve J. Spears, 1980
Performing rights enquiries should be addressed to
M & L Casting Consultants Pty Ltd
49 Darlinghurst Road, Kings Cross, NSW 2011

The Father We Loved on a Beach by the Sea © Stephen
Sewell, 1980
Performing rights enquiries should be addressed to
M & L Casting Consultants Pty Ltd
49 Darlinghurst Road, Kings Cross, NSW 2011

Irish Stew © John Bradley, 1980
Performing rights enquiries should be addressed to
Brisbane Repertory's La Boite Theatre
57 Hale Street, Brisbane, Queensland 4000

Typeset by Press Etching Pty Ltd, Brisbane
Printed and bound by Southwood Press Pty Ltd, Sydney

Distributed in the United Kingdom, Europe, the Middle
East, Africa, and the Caribbean by Prentice-Hall
International, International Book Distributors Ltd,
66 Wood Lane End, Hemel Hempstead, Herts., England

Published with the assistance of the Literature Board of the
Australia Council

National Library of Australia
Cataloguing-in-Publication data

Three political plays.

(Contemporary Australian plays; 9 ISSN 0589-7468)
Contents: King Richard/by Steve J. Spears. The father
we loved on a beach by the sea/by Steve Sewell. Irish
Stew/by John Bradley.
ISBN 0 7022 1439 6
ISBN 0 7022 1449 3 Paperback

1. Australian drama. I. Sykes, Alrene Maude, ed.
II. Spears, Steve J. King Richard. III. Sewell, Steve.
The father we loved on a beach by the sea. IV. Bradley,
John. Irish stew. V. Title: King Richard. VI. Title: The
father we loved on a beach by the sea. VII. Title: Irish
stew.

A822.3'08

Contents

p. 49-50

Foreword

These are three interesting plays, all with strong political themes. Toughly and unapologetically, the playwrights confront the injustices of our socio-political system and, in all cases, I regret to find, they are pessimistic of the chances of good prevailing over corruption and the naked power of fools.

Steve Spears in *King Richard* presents a rather raw commentary on contemporary politics. Perhaps it's a shame that a young man should be so sceptical, if not cynical about our political processes, but it's no wonder in the light of contemporary political affairs.

Stephen Sewell's *The Father We Loved on a Beach by the Sea* contrasts the hopeless "buckling under" of a father to a coersive system, and his rebellious sons whose protest is determined and persistent but finally ineffectual. The father conforms and survives, but at the cost of the independence of his personality. The sons resist at the cost of their freedom of development. As with Spears's work, there is an overwhelming sense of futility at a loaded social and political system.

Finally, there is John Bradley's *Irish Stew* which is rollicking pathos, if that is not too strong a contradiction in words. Bradley uses a seemingly purposeless ferry hijack as an allegorical illustration of how well-meaning men, who wanted to be free and to free others, took command of a system they did not understand and therefore could not control.

These are fascinating plays, stimulating in a stark and compelling way, from writers with a lot more to say yet.

BILL HAYDEN

Editor's Introduction

Very few Australian political plays have, to date, been published
— probably because, with most of them, the message is of
primary importance and the play merely a vehicle. The three
plays in this book, varied in style and outlook, are indeed
politically committed, but they have also proved in production to
be provocative, entertaining, and sometimes moving to audiences
that do not necessarily share their political vision.

Steve Spears's *King Richard* wears its political comment
lightly; it is a play of fast-moving action occasionally erupting
into knockabout farce, and with lively cynicism takes for granted
that politicians and convicted criminals can be equally corrupt
when power is their mutual goal. "King Richard" is a convicted
murderer who leads his fellow convicts out on strike, demanding
that if they manufacture an automobile anti-pollution device,
they must be paid union award wages. At first he seems to be
successful and even browbeats the premier into allowing him a
month's stay in a first-class hotel, all luxuries provided.

The Father We Loved on a Beach by the Sea is a more fiercely
committed play, which contrasts a father — unsuccessful, sub-
missive, helpless, cliche-ridden in word and deed — with his
rebellious and politically anarchic sons, in a world rigid with
fascist-style government. In the La Boite production, one was
impressed by an unusual combination of fierce political feeling
with compassion and understanding of the characters, even those
of whom one would not have expected the young author to
"approve". Stephen Sewell is still at the beginning of his play-
writing career, and it is far too early to generalize about his style,
but it is perhaps significant that several of the highly favourable
reviews of his second play, *Traitors* (first performed in
Melbourne by the APG on 19 April 1979) also commented on
Sewell's feeling for humanity as well as for politics, or as

Leonard Radic expressed it, the "author's feelings for character and for human (as distinct from narrowly political) drama."[1] The unforgettable image of *The Father We Loved* is the final one: a defeated man, standing on a beach with a child's bucket in his hand, looking out to sea.

Irish Stew is the most complex of the three plays, its mood shifting from the high comedy of an Irish joke to black bewilderment bordering on the absurd, and its dialogue packed with implication and undertone. The play lends itself to stunning visual effects, the most obviously dramatic being the moment when, at the end of the play, jet planes roar in to strafe and finally sink the ferry. (The director Sean Mee comments that he would love to see a film of the play, with full surreal effects as the ship spins in its whirlpool). The marauding jets are not defined, either by nationality or political persuasion. Many of the more recent Australian playwrights are turning away from precise nationalism (all three plays in this volume could be set elsewhere without serious dislocation), and John Bradley says firmly: "This play is international in setting, and I hope to be able to do this for ever."

Louis Nowra once commented, "It is difficult for any author to talk about his own work, for there is a crucial problem of detachment... so treat what I have to say with a degree of scepticism. Always trust the text, never the author's justification for it."[2] He then proceeded to give a brilliant and illuminating exposition of his own *Inner Voices*. Many playwrights find it difficult to talk about their own work, and are obviously justified in saying, "But it is all there in the play." On the other hand, a director may well choose to make his own interpretation of a play, whatever the playwright intended. For those directors (and readers) who are concerned to know the author's intentions, a few authorial comments, if the playwright can be persuaded to make them, may save massive misinterpretation. In a section at the end of this book the playwrights have contributed biographical notes and comments on their own plays.

King Richard, The Father We Loved on a Beach by the Sea, and *Irish Stew* all had their première performances in Brisbane's Repertory Theatre, better known as La Boite. This theatre has a long history of encouraging local writers and of providing stimulating and often controversial theatre. It was first formed in 1925, as an amateur theatre and the first Little Theatre in Brisbane; over the years it played in halls and theatres in many parts of the city but in 1972 moved into its own building, a delightful and award-winning theatre-in-the-round — La Boite — seating two hundred people and capable of transformation into thrust staging with the removal of one of the four banks of seats. At the time of writing, the theatre is a mixture of professional and amateur, the professional staff including an artistic director and business and production managers.

In 1978 Barry Oakley wrote: "If the frontiers of Brisbane's drama are going to be extended it's in La Boite's little space that it will happen."[3] La Boite's support of the three plays in this volume has been such an extension of the frontiers.

ALRENE SYKES
University of Queensland

Notes

1. "When Revolution Turns Sour", *Age,* 1 May 1979.
2. Lecture to students at the University of Queensland, 3 April 1979.
3. "Flight across the Frontier", *National Times,* 13-19 February 1978.

King Richard

Steve J. Spears

There is no other way
Unless though couldst put on some other shape
And not be Richard that hath done all this.

KING RICHARD III

Dedicated to Gough Whitlam, who lost the game to fools. And to the Mr Browns of the world who are already looking long and hard at the farmer who would be king.

Geoff Hiscock, seated("King"Richard Brown), Joe Podosky (Cobble), Brian Rigg (Dundon), and Normunds Buivids (Harris) in a scene from the La Boite premiere of *King Richard*.

King Richard was first performed at La Boite Theatre, Brisbane (by arrangement with the Old Tote Theatre Company and the Rock Theatre of Paris) on 22 September 1978, with the following cast:

"KING" RICHARD BROWN, a prisoner	Geoff Hiscock
SIR JAMES DUNDON, Premier of Victoria	Brian Rigg
DET. SGT. HARRIS	Normunds Buivids
STUART COBBLE, Premier's personal secretary	Joe Podosky
SUE, a maid	Sorrel Edwards
TONY BAILLETTI	Jim Porter
POLICEMEN	Terry Roberts
	John Nugent

Directed by Sean Mee

ACT I

A penthouse suite in a top Melbourne hotel. It is a very ritzy, plush lounge-room. Centre stage at the back is the main door which leads into the room from the corridor. A door P leads to the main (unseen) bedroom. A door OP leads to the second bedroom. A man (HARRIS) *enters. He is a plain-clothes cop with sunglasses; very big and thuggy. He quickly and expertly checks out the lounge-room for bugs or bombs or something. He beckons another man* (RICHARD BROWN) *to enter.* BROWN *is a very big man with a severe crew cut, dressed in a Prisoners' Aid Suit. He has an air of authority and calm.*

HARRIS: Enter King Richard. I hope you find this all to your satisfaction. [*Bows.*]

[BROWN, *amused, says nothing.*]

[*Flitting around room*] Ah. What have we here? Hmmm? Dimple Scotch. Very nice. Ohhhh. [*Picks up two expensive glasses.*] Crystal goblets! For my liege. [*Throws back curtain to reveal morning sunlight over Melbourne.*] Well, this is a bit better than solitary confinement, don't you think, Brown? Or do they call it protective desocialization now?

[BROWN *smiles.*]

Is there anything I can do for you, Brown?

[BROWN *lifts up his arms. His hands are cuffed.*]

No. I think not, Brown. Just a precaution. We wouldn't want the premier to get nervous, would we? Not with a big, evil man like you around. Hmmm? [*Pause.*] How long are you in for this time, Brown? Of course! Life, isn't it? [*With mock sympathy*] Ohhh. Now I remember. You went and killed a few people, that right? Yes. [*Counts on fingers.*] One, an inspector. Two, a detective sergeant. Three, a police constable. That was all, wasn't it? Oh, pardon me. Of course, you killed a police dog too, didn't you? It slipped my mind. Did you kick the dog to death, Brown?

BROWN: No. I strangled him, Harris.

HARRIS: Mother Mary! [*In mock surprise*] You strangled an Alsatian doggie! You must be *strong.* [*Pause.*] I say you must be strong, Brown, hmmm? To kill three policemen and then top it off by choking a dog to death. Hmmm? You pretty strong Richard? Hmmm? Plenty muscles, huh?

[HARRIS *has been getting madder as* BROWN *fails to rise to the bait. He pours two Dimples, approaches* BROWN, *and offers him one.* BROWN *remains immobile. They look at each other for a long time,* HARRIS *holding the Scotch out eagerly.*]

Drink, Brown? [*Pause.*] Brown, I'm offering you a drink. Hmmm? *Hey!* Don't you stand there and ignore *me,* pal. I'm offering you a fucking drink! Take it! *Hey!* Take it!

[BROWN *wearily reaches for the drink.* HARRIS *pulls it back from his reach and throws it in* BROWN'S *face.*]

Holy Jesus! I spilt the drink, Brown. Did you see that? [*Silence.*] [*Worried*] Brown, I'm talking to you. I said I spilt the drink. Did you see?

BROWN: Yes Harris, I saw.

HARRIS: I hope you don't think I did that deliberately. [*Silence.*] I say, Brown, [*loudly*] I hope you don't think I did that on purpose!

BROWN: Listen, Harris, forget all this, will you? Just stop it.

HARRIS: "Just stop it." [*Schoolmaster voice*] I say, you there, Harris. I'm getting terribly fed up with this misbehaviour. Just stop it. [*Pause.*] You're boss stuff, Brown, you know that? Boss stuff. [*Punches him on arm.*] They don't make them any tougher than King Richard. That right?

BROWN: That's right, Harris.

HARRIS: Uh uh. That's wrong, Harris. That's wrong, Harris. Tell you why that's wrong, Harris. That's wrong because I'm not Harris. No sir. I'm Detective Sergeant Harris. I'm Mister Harris. So I guess that's wrong, Harris. Hmmm?
[*Silence.*]
Richard, pet. I'm talking to you. [*He puts his hand around the back of* BROWN'S *head.*] [*Distinctly into* BROWN'S *face*] I said: I guess that's wrong, Mister Harris. Do you agree?

BROWN [*looks blankfaced into* HARRIS'S *face*]: Yes. That's wrong, Mister Harris.

HARRIS: Well, thank heavens, that's settled! Now, how about another drink? [*He offers his drink to* BROWN. BROWN *takes it.*] Ooooo. Tsk. What do we say?

BROWN: We say, "Thank you, Mister Harris." We say, "Yes sir." We say, "Shove this up your arse, you syphilitic pig fucker."
[BROWN *spits a large mouthful into* HARRIS'S *face.* HARRIS *throws a punch at* BROWN, *who sidesteps and grabs* HARRIS'S *arm, kicking him in the ribs.* HARRIS *falls to the ground.*

[BROWN *picks up a piece of furniture to throw at* HARRIS, *who has pulled out his gun.* BROWN *regretfully puts the furniture down.*]

[*Silence.*]

HARRIS: Got ya.

BROWN: Yes.

HARRIS: You attacked a police officer, Brown.

BROWN: Yes.

[*Silence.*]

[*Phone rings.*]

HARRIS: Excuse me. [*Slams* BROWN *on the shoulder with the gun.*] [*Into phone*] Penthouse suite. [*Pause.*] Thank you. [*To* BROWN] The premier is on his way up. [*Pause.*] You all right?

BROWN: Yes.

HARRIS: I don't like you, Brown. I don't like people who kill policemen. We're just human beings, you know.

[BROWN *shrugs.*]

[*Doorbell rings.* HARRIS *answers it.*]

[*The premier of Victoria,* SIR JAMES DUNDON, *enters with male secretary,* STUART COBBLE.]

HARRIS: Good morning, Mr Premier.

DUNDON: Good morning. Who are you?

HARRIS: Detective Sergeant Harris, sir. Twenty-seven Squad.

DUNDON: Does er . . . [*beckons* HARRIS *away to corner.*]

[*They speak in whispers, glancing now and then at* BROWN, *who pours himself a large Scotch. Finally:*]

Fine, fine. [*Approaches* BROWN.] How do you do, Brown.

BROWN: G'day.

DUNDON: I see. You want to play it that way, do you? [*No answer.*] Harris, is this man deaf?

HARRIS: No, Mr Premier, he's a trouble-maker.

DUNDON: Yes. Yes. [*He snaps his fingers at* STUART, *who produces a folder. He leafs through it.*] Well. [*Looks at* BROWN *in amusement.*] A dog? It's not a very impressive record, is it? Not very impressive.

BROWN: I did my best.

HARRIS: Shut up, Brown! All right! This man is the premier of Victoria!

DUNDON: It's OK, sergeant. Look — um — Brown, let's stop the bullshit, what do you say? I've set up this meeting for a reason. Let's just get on with it. I'm a busy man, a busy man. [*Takes* The Age *from* STUART.] Now read this.

HARRIS: Brown can't read, sir.

DUNDON: I should have known. Stuart, read it out for him, will you?

STUART: Which part, sir?

DUNDON: The whole bloody thing!

STUART: Yes sir. Well — um — Mr Brown . . . the headline [*showing* BROWN *the headline*] just here . . . see? . . . says —

DUNDON: Christ Almighty! Stuart! This isn't Romper Room. Read what it says!

STUART: Yes sir. The headline says: Convict union on strike. It's subtitled: Defiant prisoners riot in four states. Then there's a picture of you, Mr Brown. . . .

BROWN: Where?

STUART: Just here. [*Shows* BROWN.] It goes on. . . .

BROWN: Terrible picture.

STUART [*studying it*]: Yes. It makes your ears look . . . [*Flutters hands about his ears.*] er — er—

BROWN: Like cauliflower ears.

STUART: That's it, yes. Yes. Like a boxer or something.

DUNDON: Stuart?

STUART: Yes, Mr Premier?

DUNDON: May I have a look? [*Holds out hand.*]

STUART: Yes sir.

DUNDON [*studying it*]: Yes. I see what you mean. It does make his ears look squashed, doesn't it?

STUART [*sensing trouble*]: Yes sir.

DUNDON: It's probably the lighting, don't you think?

STUART: I don't know, sir.

DUNDON: I think it is. I think they didn't light up the side of his head enough, and it made his ears go . . . [*Imitates* STUART'S *hand flutter.*] er — shadowy. I'm bit of an amateur photographer actually.

STUART: Are you?

DUNDON: Yes.

STUART: Yes.

DUNDON: Stuart?

STUART: Yes sir.

DUNDON: Is that all you'd like to say about this photograph? [STUART *nods.*]

Sure? O.K. Would — um — you like to go on with your reading?

STUART: It goes on. . . .

DUNDON: It might be an idea to start again.

STUART: Yes sir. Well. [*Clears his throat.*] The headline says: Convict union on strike. The subtitle is: Defiant prisoners riot in four states. Then — er — as I said, there's a picture of Mr Brown. It goes on . . . um . . . parenthesis King — that's — er — inverted commas King — Richard Brown, the head of the self-styled Union of Australian Convicts, has ordered all prison inmates not to leave their cells in the third Australia-wide strike by prisoners since June 1977. Authoritative sources have confirmed that King Richard Brown — convicted triple murderer — has called the strike in protest against the Victorian government's plans to involve the prisoners in the manufacture of the new Von Arnim anti-pollution devices. The premier of Victoria, Sir James Dundon, said last night at a special press conference, that the state government would never recognize the, quote, fallacious notion that murderers, thieves, and other convicted enemies of society are entitled to band together under the bogus title of a union. Richard Brown, he went on to say, is just another convict as far as the government and the majority of right-thinking Victorians are concerned. He pledged that he would never back down to pressure from a few misfits and that the Von Arnim devices would be built by the prisoners *in* the prisons. . . .

DUNDON: OK, Stuart. I think Mr Brown has the general idea. [*To* BROWN] Well, you can see my position. I have publicly stated one thing, and you have publicly stated the exact opposite. What we have here is, in those immortal words, a failure to communicate. We have a conflict. I want it resolved. [*He looks expectantly at* BROWN, *who impassively looks right back.*] Um, Brown, you have a very disturbing habit of not answering people.

BROWN: What's the question?

DUNDON: The question is: Will you call off this ridiculous charade and get your convict friends back to work on the Von Arnim devices?

BROWN [*indicating handcuffs*]: Take these off.

DUNDON: Brown, damn you, I want an answer!

BROWN: I'll give you an answer when you take these off.
    [*Long pause.*]
DUNDON: Harris. Remove his handcuffs.
HARRIS: It's not a wise idea, sir. He's an unpredictable boy.
DUNDON: Just shut up and do as you're told.
HARRIS: Yes, Mr Premier. [*He removes* BROWN'S *handcuffs.*] [*To*
    BROWN] Now you just behave yourself, Richard.
DUNDON: Well?
BROWN: Well, the answer to your question is maybe.
DUNDON: Brown, you're trying my patience. [*Pause.*] Your
    answer is no answer. *Maybe* you'll call off the strike.
BROWN: That's right. Maybe I will.
DUNDON: Incredible. And please tell me, if you don't mind, what it
    is that will make your mind up for you. Money? Is that it?
    You want money? An early parole? What do you want?
BROWN: I want what you want, Mr Premier.
DUNDON: What on earth are you talking about?
BROWN: I'm a realistic man, I don't have the power you have. I
    can't get what I want. You have the power to give it to me,
    but you won't.
DUNDON: What?
BROWN: We want your government to accept our log of claims.
    The Union of Australian Convicts feels that, if they are to
    be employed as assembly-line workers, then we should be
    paid the award rate. This stand has been backed by the
    CPA, the MWU, and most of the major unions.
DUNDON: You're right, you know, Brown.
BROWN: Hmmm?
DUNDON: You're right. It is within my power to give you all those
    things. But I won't.
BROWN: Well, as I said Dundon, I'm a realistic —
HARRIS: Watch your mouth, Brown!
BROWN [*to* HARRIS]: I've had enough of you, Harris. Get out.
HARRIS: Woooooo. You're stupid, Brown, stu*pid*. [*He starts to*
    approach BROWN.]
DUNDON: Stay where you are, Harris.
HARRIS: No sir. I've had it with this fool. I —
DUNDON: Shut the fuck *up,* Harris!
    [*Pause.*]
HARRIS: Yes sir.
BROWN: I want an apology from him.
HARRIS: What?

BROWN: I said I want you to apologize to me.

DUNDON: You're being ridiculous, Brown.

[BROWN *gestures "That's your opinion."*]

[*Rising*] Come on, Stuart. I think we've wasted enough time. Goodbye.

[DUNDON *and* STUART *exit.*]

[BROWN *sits impassively.* HARRIS *looks at him with bemusement.*]

HARRIS: Oh, King Richard. You messed that up. You missed the beat. [*Pause.*] Ooooooo boy. You missed that beat by *so* many miles. You nearly had it, didn't you. You nearly had the Big Boys right there at your feet. ... Oh, please Mr Brown, please please make these terrible strikes go away. Oh, we'll do what you want, only please please please help us. [*Taps head.*] You're stupid. [*Pause.*] Stand up.

[BROWN *stands up.* HARRIS *tosses him the handcuffs.* BROWN *starts to put them on.*]

No, Brown, round the back.

[BROWN *resignedly fastens the cuffs behind his back.* HARRIS *looks at him. Long silence.*]

[*Doorbell rings.* HARRIS, *surprised, goes to door.*]

HARRIS: Who's there?

DUNDON [*from behind door*]: Open it up, Harris.

[HARRIS *opens the door.* DUNDON *and* STUART *enter.* DUNDON *approaches* BROWN.]

DUNDON: Well?

BROWN: Donleavy Enterprises.

DUNDON [*smiles*]: I *knew* it. [*Pause.*] Well.

BROWN [*indicating handcuffs*]: Take these off.

DUNDON: Harris. Um — take those things off, will you?

[HARRIS, *confused, reluctantly takes the cuffs off.*]

BROWN: I want an apology from him.

DUNDON: Harris. . . .

HARRIS: You've got to be —

DUNDON: I haven't got time to play games. He wants an apology. Give it to him.

HARRIS: No.

DUNDON: Harris. Damn you! I don't have time. Apologize. [*Silence.*] Jesus Christ! If [*slowly*] ... if you want your job, just do what I tell you.

[HARRIS *mumbles something.*]

BROWN: I didn't hear you, Harris.

HARRIS: I said, I apologize.

BROWN: Stuart, did you hear what Mr Harris said?

STUART: Yes. He said, I apologize.

BROWN: Who do you think he was talking to?

STUART: Um — to you, I suppose.

BROWN: Yes. I suppose he was. Were you talking to me, Harris?
[*Silence.*]

DUNDON [*shouting*]: Answer him!

HARRIS: Yes.

BROWN: Then would you please —

HARRIS [*interrupting*]: I apologize, Mr Brown.

BROWN: Thank heavens that's settled! Now get out.
[HARRIS *looks at* DUNDON, *who nods.* HARRIS *shrugs and exits.*]

DUNDON: Stuart. Get onto the commissioner. I want him [*indicating* HARRIS] fired.

STUART: Yes sir. [*Picks up phone.*]

DUNDON: Use the phone in the bedroom, please.

STUART: Yes sir. [*Exits to bedroom. Closes the door.*]

DUNDON: Sit down, Brown.
[*They sit down.*]

BROWN: I want to stay here.

DUNDON: Where?

BROWN: Here in this suite.

DUNDON: What? Why?

BROWN: I like it better than Pentridge.

DUNDON: You want to spend the rest of your sentence here? What would that be? Another thirty years?

BROWN: No. I want to stay here for a month. Regardless of the outcome of our talk. As a — um — gesture of good will.

DUNDON: You're a strange man, Brown. [*Pause. Shrugs.*] OK. If you like.

BROWN: Good. [*Moves to table. Picks up pen and paper.*] Would you — er . . .?

DUNDON: Of course. You can't write. What do you want me to say?

BROWN: It's addressed to Anthony Bailletti. I want it delivered this afternoon. Um — Tony. Will be spending about a month away from Pentridge. Pass the word around the union that I'm all right and there's no cause for any action. Richard Brown. And write the number sixty-nine at the bottom.

DUNDON: What's sixty-nine for?

BROWN: It's a code number. It means that the message is genuine.

DUNDON: Oooo, very exciting.

[*They sit down.*]

What do you know about Donleavy Enterprises?

BROWN: Dundon, we're speaking like children. It doesn't really matter how much I know. The important thing is that I think you may want me and my union to — er — do certain things that are at variance with certain public statements you've made.

DUNDON: I see. What do you think I want your — um — union to do?

BROWN: I don't know.

DUNDON: Well, I'll tell you. I've said it in parliament, I've said it on the television and whatnot. I want all Victorian prisoners to get to work on the Von Arnim devices. I want them *out* of their cells, off their bottoms, and back on the assembly line.

[BROWN *looks at him impassively.*]

Brown! I want those devices. I want them freely available at the lowest price possible. I want them to be here in my state *first*. I want them made and I want them made new.

[BROWN *looks impassive.*]

[*smiles*]: That's an old trick, Brown. I use it myself. Look at people long enough like this [*Makes stonewall face.*] and they'll blow their own brains out just to get a reaction. Right?

BROWN: Would you like a drink?

DUNDON: Thank you. The Dimple, I think.

BROWN [*pouring drinks*]: You think these Von Arnim devices really work?

DUNDON: Of course they work, man. We've made every conceivable test. They are absolutely amazing. The worst — [*Takes drink from* BROWN.] thank you — the *worst* result we got was a kilometre-per-gallon reduction of thirty per cent and a carbon monoxide and lead oxide pollution reduction of *fifty-five* per cent. And in most cases the results were very much much better. Petrol reduction and pollution — well — eradication virtually with one simple little device.

BROWN: So what?

DUNDON: So what? Come off it, Brown. I —

BROWN: Don't tell me — you care for the environment.

DUNDON: Damn right I care for the environment. I have three kids, you know. I want them to inherit a *world,* not a morgue.

BROWN: Hmmm. I want to meet him.

DUNDON [*exasperated*]: You want to meet whom?

BROWN: I want to meet the man who designed the device. I want to meet Mr Von Arnim.

DUNDON [*putting hands over face*]: Hahahahaha.
    [STUART *enters tentatively from bedroom.*]

STUART: Excuse me, Mr Premier — um — I spoke to the commissioner. He would prefer not to fire Sergeant Harris. He said. . . .

DUNDON: What did he say, Stuart?

STUART: Well, sir, he said that he regards Harris as a good policeman. And he wondered whether it might be possible instead to take him out of the picture for a while.

DUNDON [*amused*]: Does he want the Premier's Department to kidnap him?

STUART [*sniggering*]: Oh no. Dear me, no sir. He suggested that one of the — um — police exchange schemes that we have with Singapore might . . .

DUNDON: I see. All right. Get him into one of those, then. I don't want to *see* him for at least six months, OK? And tell the commissioner to make sure Harris is out of Australia by midnight.

STUART: Yes sir. Oh — um — he seemed quite upset on the phone.

DUNDON [*annoyed*]: Oh, Jesus. All right. Ring him back, convey my apologies, et cetera et cetera. Stress that it *is* important. Tell him, tell him my piles are playing up again and that I'll get on to him as soon as — er — tomorrow morning.

STUART: Yes sir. [*Exits to bedroom.*]
    [*Pause.*]

DUNDON: Hmmmm. Now, where were we?

BROWN: I want to see Von Arnim.

DUNDON: Out of the question.

BROWN: Then we have nothing further to discuss.

DUNDON: I don't understand you, Brown. What does it matter if the devices work or not.

BROWN: You've already answered that question.

DUNDON: You must see that you put me in an impossible situation. How would it look to the media if I were to be seen kowtowing to the whims of the president of a union that I deny even exists and further to a man who is a convicted triple murderer? Hmmm?

BROWN: You have my word that I will not divulge anything about this affair to the media.

DUNDON [*amused*]: Your word.

BROWN: Yes.

DUNDON: OK. [*Laughs.*] Jesus. OK, OK, I'll trust you. I'll arrange for Von Arnim to come here as soon as possible.

BROWN: Tomorrow

DUNDON [*quietly*]: Don't push too hard, King Richard. I have a big stick.

BROWN: Yes. I've felt your stick.

[*Pause.*]

DUNDON: OK. Tomorrow. He'll bring the plans, test results, the works. You'll find they're good. It's a wonderful machine, Brown, a wonderful machine.

BROWN: Yes. If all I've heard is true, it'll be a great benefit.

DUNDON: Not just to Victoria. To the world.

BROWN: Yes.

[*They contemplate in silence.*]

[STUART *enters.*]

STUART: Um — excuse me, Mr Premier, Mr Brown. Um — the commissioner said that he'll fix up the Harris thing. He wants to know if you'll be requiring another plain-clothes from the Twenty-seven Squad.

DUNDON: No. They're too corrupt. Tell him to send a man from Gaming. [*Looks at* BROWN.] Make that two men. Get them here fast.

STUART: Yes sir. [*Exits to bedroom.*]

DUNDON: Why are we arguing? We're of the same mind. The Von Arnims are everything they're made out to be. Why won't your prisoners build them?

BROWN: Because I told them not to.

DUNDON: Dunstan and Bjelke-Petersen have made the same requests. Why won't your prisoners build them?

BROWN: Because I told them not to.

DUNDON: Yes yes. Why?

BROWN: Look, we've published our log of claims. You know what we want. Why are you bandying words with me?

DUNDON: I suppose I'm curious. You know, don't you, that if you persist with these demands, the contract will go to private enterprise and your men will go back to doing government laundry and making mailbags? You must realize that these wage claims are totally unacceptable.

BROWN: Then why did you want to see me?

DUNDON: To change your mind.

BROWN: Really? Do you really want to change my mind, Mr Premier?

DUNDON: Of course I do. If this stalemate continues . . .

BROWN: My information is that Donleavy Enterprises wants the Von Arnim contract.

DUNDON: Get to the point.

BROWN: I've gotten there. Donleavy Enterprises. . . .

DUNDON: Look, Brown, GMH, Ford, everyone and his dog wants the contract.

BROWN: Yes indeed. It might be profitable.

[*Pause.*]

DUNDON: I don't like the turn of this conversation, Brown. Put your cards down.

BROWN: No.

DUNDON: Brown. You're an infuriating man. You know — correction — you *think* you know something about me. Some juicy little scandal? Hmmm?

BROWN: Dundon, if I told you all I knew about you and your sleazy little dealings, I think you'd — um — put me out of the picture.

DUNDON: They don't have overseas exchange schemes for prisoners.

BROWN: I know.

DUNDON: Tell me more, Brown. Come on. Tell me about my sleazy little dealings.

BROWN: I've already said more than I intended. You have a gift for drawing people out, Dundon.

DUNDON [*looking at watch*]: Shit, I'm late. [*Stands.*] Stuart!

[STUART *enters from bedroom.*]

[*To* BROWN] Well, what's your answer?

BROWN: Sit down.

[DUNDON *sits down with infinite patience.*]

Here's my answer. I don't know whether I'll call off the strike. It depends on a number of things. It depends on what this Von Arnim has to say, whether the devices are good. I want what's best for my union and myself.

DUNDON [*triumphant*]: Aha! I was waiting —

BROWN: Shhhhhh. I want what's best for my union and myself. I want what you want, Mr Premier. We *are,* as you say, of one mind in this matter. Today is the second. You'll have my answer by the thirtieth.

DUNDON: No. I'll want your answer tomorrow. That's imperative. I want it tomorrow or this whole [*indicating room*] deal is off.

BROWN: Then we have nothing further to discuss.

DUNDON: Nothing to discuss! You damn fool! Don't you know I can just send in the fucking *army* and make your precious cons work? I've wasted half a morning trying to talk sense into you, and all you can say is, I want this. I want that. Fuck you, Brown! *I* want. I'm not asking, I'm not negotiating, I'm ordering you and your clowns to get out of your cells and back to work. Right?

BROWN: Maybe.

[DUNDON *looks at* BROWN *in amazement.*]

Stuart. Go back into the bedroom, please.

STUART: Yes sir. [*Goes to exit.*]

DUNDON: Stuart! Don't you *dare* take one more step.

BROWN: Go.

DUNDON: You'll be quiet!

[BROWN *looks at* DUNDON, *then lightly slaps him across the face. He shoves* STUART *roughly into the bedroom, closing the door. He moves quickly to the front door and wedges a chair under the handle. Hammering and noises on outside of door.*]

[BROWN *picks up phone.*]

BROWN [*into phone*]: Stuart, put down the phone, please. [*Waits till satisfied.*] [*To* DUNDON, *petrified*] Listen, Dundon. I know what game you're playing with Donleavy, and I don't like it. You will have my answer in four weeks. Until then, I'll stay here. Not in Pentridge. Here. [*Picks up phone.*] Stuart, I won't tell you again. [*Waits till satisfied.*] You will let me have the things I want and not argue about it. I give you my word I won't escape, nor will I contact anyone while I'm here. I want this month, *capice? I want* it.

DUNDON: OK.

BROWN: I want no guards or bugging devices in my room.

DUNDON: I'll have to post men outside.

BROWN: They are not to enter.

DUNDON: Agreed.

BROWN: I want the phones left connected.

DUNDON: Only if my men can monitor the calls.

BROWN: Agreed. I want unlimited credit through room service. Agreed?

[DUNDON *nods.*]

My friend in Pentridge, Anthony Bailletti, I want him brought here for the month.

DUNDON: No.

BROWN: Yes.

DUNDON: No. That's not possible.

BROWN: It is possible.

DUNDON: You're pushing too hard, Richard.

BROWN: I need Bailletti. I need him to read for me.

DUNDON: Can you guarantee his silence?

BROWN: Yes.

DUNDON: Very well.

BROWN [*taking* DUNDON'S *hand*]: It's a pleasure doing business with you, Mr Premier.

[BROWN *opens bedroom door.* STUART *cautiously enters.*]

STUART: Are you all right, sir?

DUNDON: Certainly, Stuart. Mr Brown and I had some further business to discuss. [*Indicating noise at front door*] Shut them up, would you?

[STUART *does so.*]

[*To* BROWN] I'll have to make arrangements. You understand the phone will be turned off till the — er — tap is put on.

BROWN: Fine. How long will that take?

DUNDON: Ooooo. Two hours. Three at the outside.

BROWN: Good. Stuart?

[BROWN *moves to writing table. Picks up letter.*]

This is the letter to Bailletti?

[DUNDON *nods.*]

[*To* STUART]

Read it out, please.

STUART [*puzzled*]: Hickory dickory dock, the mouse ran up the clock. . . .

[BROWN *approaches* DUNDON.]

BROWN [*quietly*]: Do you remember what the message was?

DUNDON: Ahem. Yes.

BROWN: Will you have it relayed to Bailletti?

DUNDON: Yes.

BROWN: Don't forget the code number.

DUNDON: No.

[*Pause.*]

BROWN: I won't see you again.

DUNDON: Of course you'll see me again. [*Offers hand.*] Au revoir.

BROWN [*shakes*]: Goodbye.

[DUNDON *exits.* STUART *is about to exit.*]

Oh Stuart. Get room service to find the best tailor in town. I want him up here at two.

STUART: A tailor, Mr Brown?

BROWN: Yes. Tell him to bring shoes.

STUART: Shoes?

BROWN: Size twelve.

STUART: Size twelve. Is this all all right with the premier?

BROWN: Oh yes. [*Pinches* STUART'S *cheek.*] I got him, Stuart; I got him by the balls.

DUNDON [*from down the corridor*]: Hurry up! You idiot!

STUART [*yelling*]: Coming sir! [*Exits.*]

[BROWN *wanders round the room playing with all the goodies like a child, smiling.*]

END OF ACT I

ACT II

The next day. Mid morning. BROWN *is dressed in an expensive dressing gown. He has just finished a plush breakfast. He lights up a plush smoke. He picks up the phone.*

BROWN: Room service? Brown. Send someone out. I want a Sony stereo cassette; TC161SD. No, make that two. [*Pause.*] Yes two. Speakers for both of them. Oh. And I want the complete set of Dylan tapes. No, *Bob* Dylan. Oh. Have the suits and clothes arrived yet? Get hold of that tailor, the one who came yesterday. Tell him I want them by eleven. Oh. Send up a crate of Southern Comfort. Yes, a crate. . . . I *know* how many bottles are in a crate. [*Pause.*] Look, friend, I'm going to be here for another month. Just do what you're told, understand? If you are in any doubt, refer to the manager, OK? Now have you got all that? Thank you.
[*Puts phone on hook. Sits down. Grins.*]
[SUE, *the maid, enters.* BROWN *looks at her quizzically. As she is reaching for the breakfast things, he grabs her wrist. She is scared. He looks at her hands.*]
You have nice hands.
[*She is scared.*]
Relax. I'm not going to bite you. Have you received any orders about me?

SUE: How do you mean?

BROWN: You brought dinner up yesterday, then you brought tea up. Then you cleared away those broken glasses last night. What time was that?

SUE: Midnight, about.

BROWN: Yes. I'm sorry. I got drunk.

SUE: I had to put you to bed.

BROWN: That was you? [*Pause.*] You work very long hours.

SUE: Yes, I do.

BROWN: Why?

SUE: How do you mean?

BROWN: Why is it that you're the only member of the hotel staff I've seen? Why is it that the cleaning maid is also the waitress? And the room service?

SUE: I must get on with my work.

BROWN: You must work twenty-four hours a day. Have you been assigned to me or something?

SUE: Um?

[*Pause.*]

BROWN: What's your name?

SUE: Sue.

BROWN: Sue. My wife's name is Sue.

SUE: You've got a *wife?*

BROWN: Sure. Even us murderers have wives.

SUE [*scared*]: I must go.

BROWN: Relax. Have you?

SUE: Have I what?

BROWN: Have you been assigned to me?

SUE: I'm not supposed to talk about it.

BROWN: Go on. Be a devil.

SUE: I'll lose my job.

BROWN: No you won't. I won't tell anyone.

[*Pause.*]

SUE: I know who you are.

BROWN: Do you?

SUE: You're Richard Brown. The killer.

BROWN: That's right.

SUE: They told me you'd be staying here for a few weeks. I'm the only staff allowed in here.

BROWN: Why?

SUE: The premier, Sir James Dundon . . . this is his own suite. He often has people in here that . . .

BROWN: That he doesn't want the rest of the hotel to know about?

SUE: Yes.

BROWN: Who *does* know I'm here?

SUE: I really shouldn't talk about it.

BROWN: Ah, go on.

SUE: Well. The manager, Mr Hardy, knows of course. And Peter and Jane in room service. I think that's all. Mr Hardy says you're an important man from overseas.

BROWN: Overseas. [*Laughs.*] I went to Tasmania once. [*Pause.*] You want some tea?

SUE: I'm not supposed to . . . [*She stops. Laughs. Nods.*]
[BROWN *pours her some tea. She sits and begins buttering some toast.*]

BROWN: What do you think of him?

SUE: Who?

BROWN: The premier.

SUE: Ummm. Well. He's the *premier.* [*Pause.*] He's a very nice man.

BROWN: He's an arsehole.

SUE: That's what I meant. He's a very nice man for an arsehole.
[*They laugh.*]

BROWN: Does he give you orders direct?

SUE: No. I've never spoken to him.

BROWN: What about Stuart?

SUE: Who? Oh, that funny little man. [*Flutters her hands.*] No.
I've only seen him once. I don't think he's ever seen me.
[*Pause.*] Mr Dundon, [*whispers*] he's tapped your phone.

BROWN [*whispers*]: I know.

SUE [*whispers*]: You know?

BROWN [*whispers*]: Yep. Why are we whispering?

SUE [*giggles*]: There's a lot of policemen here. I mean, besides
the two on your door. They've cleared the whole of the
sixteenth floor just below, and they're all living there. Mr
Hardy said he wanted them here just in case.

BROWN: In case what?

SUE: In case you murdered someone, I suppose. [*Takes more
toast.*] They've got rifles and things.
[*Pause.* BROWN *sits thinking.*]
What's she like, your wife?

BROWN: She was nice.

SUE: Oh. Is she dead?

BROWN: No. She divorced me after the ... after I killed those
cops.

SUE: Why did you kill them?

BROWN: They — well they weren't very easy men to get along with.

SUE: Oh. [*Pause.*] Where is she now?

BROWN: Woolloomooloo.

SUE: What does she do?

BROWN: She married a cat burglar.

SUE [*giggles*]: Really?

BROWN: Really.

SUE: You won't tell anyone that we talked? Promise?

BROWN: OK.

SUE: What time do you want lunch?

BROWN: If I asked you to do certain things for me, would you?

SUE [*scared*]: What sort of things?
[BROWN *takes her hand and leans close, as though to kiss
her.*]

BROWN: I don't know yet. Maybe deliver things. Letters.

SUE: I don't know. What if ...?

BROWN: They won't find out.
  [*Pause.*]
SUE: Yes. All right.
BROWN: Thank you. I can't trust anyone else. [*Pause.*] You must
  be careful. Soon, I'll be able to protect you.
SUE: I don't understand you.
BROWN [*smiles*]: Listen. Soon I'll be gone from here. Then you'll
  be safe. Anyway, don't worry about that yet. OK?
SUE: Sure.
BROWN: Keep your eyes open, will you? And stay away from
  Dundon.
SUE: But he's the *premier.*
BROWN: He's as bent as a coat-hanger. Promise me.
SUE: Yes.
BROWN [*kisses her on forehead*]: Good.
  [*The doorbell rings.*]
  What?
MAN'S VOICE: Room service.
BROWN: Come in.
  [*Two thuggy cops bring in two cassette players. They take
  them out of the cartons and check them very carefully as*
  SUE *packs up the breakfast things and exits. The cops
  mumble about guns and hidden compartments, etc.
  Finally:*]
COP 1: There you are, King Richard. The goods you ordered.
BROWN: Thanks. You boys on the door, are you?
COP 1: Yes sir.
BROWN: I hope you like Bob Dylan. I plan to play him.
COP 1: Excellent. Good-day to you.
BROWN: And good-day to you, officers. Oh, would you ...?
  [*Gestures vaguely to the cartons and paper on the floor.*]
  [*The cops, with mounting fury, pick them up and exit.*]
  [BROWN *fiddles about with the Sony. Plays some Dylan.
  Sits on the floor, listening, his back to the door.*]
  [COP 2 *shows* TONY BAILLETTI *into the room.* TONY *looks
  around appreciatively. He is dressed in a Prisoners' Aid
  suit. He mimes sneaking up on* BROWN, *who seems unaware.
  As* TONY *is about to say boo,* BROWN *switches off the
  cassette.*]
BROWN: Tony. How are you?
TONY: Just *once,* King, just *once* I'm going to beat you. I'll throw a
  party.

[BROWN *smiles, grabs* TONY *affectionately by the shoulders. Moves to door. Swings it open.*
Two cops are there with champagne glasses, listening.]

BROWN: Check with Dundon, boys. There's to be no eaves-dropping, all right. Go on. . . . shoo!

COP 1: Some day I'm going to kick your teeth in, Brown.

[BROWN *looks at him for a moment. Insolent. Slams the door in their faces. Thinking.*]

TONY: So?

BROWN: Hmmm.

TONY: Tell me what's happening! Last night I was in my nice warm cell, then some cops drive me to this lousy lice-infested penthouse. So?

BROWN [*slightly agitated*]: I shouldn't have brought you, Tony. I didn't know. I shouldn't have brought you.

TONY: Shouldn't have brought me? Hey, King. I was unny joking. I don't mind this place at all.

BROWN: Yeah. Well, it's too late. [*Slaps him affectionately.*]
[*The doorbell rings.*]
What?

COP 1 [*opening door*]: Your tailor's outside.

TONY: Your tailor!

BROWN: I haven't got time to see him. Tell him to leave the stuff with room service and get it sent up. And tell them to hurry up with the Southern Comfort.
[COP 1 *slams door.*]
Tony. Put that speaker up near the door.
[TONY *puts speaker next to door.* BROWN *puts on some Dylan, soft.*]

BROWN: Tony. I want you to rig a tap on that phone.

TONY: Sure. [*Picks it up.*] Shouldn't be . . . Huh? Room service? Oh. . . . er — send up . . . send up a coconut, will you? Yes, a big brown one. Thanks very much. [*Puts phone down.*] Scared the shit outta me. Listen. That phone's already tapped.

BROWN: I know. It's tapped. . . . [*Gestures "going out".*] I want it tapped. . . . [*Gestures "coming in".*]

TONY: Sure. We'll need some stuff.

BROWN: Like what?

TONY: Some — er — [*Mumbles some electronics jargon.*] Can we get it from room service?

BROWN: No.

TONY: Well. I can make it up from some parts in that [*indicating television set.*] You want it tied into that [*indicating cassette*], do you? No worries.
[*The doorbell rings.*]

BROWN: What?

COP 1 [*entering*]: Room service. Here's the clothes, sir. [*Tosses beautiful suits and shirts and shoes into a heap.*]
[COP 2 *enters with crate of Southern Comfort.* TONY *reaches into his pocket, takes out a silver coin, and tosses it to* COP 2.]

TONY: Thank you, my good man.
[COP 2 *watches the coin hit him and fall to the floor. He knocks* TONY *down and starts kicking him.*
BROWN*grabs* COP 2 *by the throat and starts choking him.*
COP 1, *who has watched this all in surprise, pulls out his gun, yelling,* "Hold on, hold on, hold on" *all the time.*
BROWN, *who has been shaking* COP 2 *like a rat, finally lets go, and* COP 2 *falls to the floor.*
COP 2 *gets up shakily and points a warning finger at* BROWN *and* TONY; *then, out of the blue, kicks out at* BROWN, *who sidesteps and shoves the cop against the wall.*
COP 1 *starts* "Hold on, hold on, hold on" *again.*
BROWN*steps away from* COP 2 *who is semi-unconscious.*
COP 1 *keeps his eyes and gun on* BROWN *as he picks up his mate and exits back-first through the door, saying stupidly,* "All right, all right, no no, all right, all right, no no", *etc. Closes door.*]
[BROWN *looks at* TONY *distastefully.* TONY *sulkily goes to the television set and starts unscrewing its back. Silence as* BROWN *watches him.*]

BROWN: How many times do I have to tell you? If you haven't got a piano, don't boogie.
[TONY *doesn't answer.* BROWN *opens up a bottle of Southern Comfort.*]

END OF ACT II

ACT III

Night time of the same day.
BROWN *and* TONY *are drunk. The television set is back in its normal place. Southern Comfort bottles are strewn around.*
BROWN *is dressed in silk shirt, suit.*
TONY [*indicating* BROWN'S *clothes*]: That's nice, King.
BROWN: Thanks.
TONY: Hey?
BROWN: Yeah.
TONY: You got everything you want, huh? Nice clothes. TV, music, [*picks up coconut*] fruit, [*picks up good quality self-developing camera*] gadgets, booze. You got everything.
[BROWN *nods, contented.*]
What's with you and that maid? She's nice.
BROWN: She's beautiful.
TONY: Yeah. [*Looks around.*] You sure got Dundon by the balls.
BROWN: No.
TONY: What are you talking about? You got him by the balls.
[BROWN *gestures "no I haven't".*]
Sure you have, King. By the nutterooooos!
[*Silence.*]
BROWN: He's making his move too soon.
TONY: What you say?
BROWN: He's making his move too soon.
TONY: Who?
BROWN: Listen, Tony. You're going to take over the union, right? You should win the election, right?
TONY: Yeah, sure I'll win it. In forty years when they let you out. Then I'll win it.
BROWN: They're going to let me out soon, paisan.
TONY: They gonna let you out! Hey that's great, King. Boy, you sure got him by the balls. Shit. They gonna let you out.
BROWN: So. You have to be good, Tony. You have to be strong. You don't use your *head* enough, sometimes, you know? You have to take *care* of the union. Understand?
TONY: Yeah. I know. When are you going, King?
[*The phone rings. Both men spring drunkenly to their posts.*
BROWN *moves to the front door, blocking it.*
TONY *plugs something into the phone, puts on cassette.*]

TONY [*into phone*]: Yeah? This is Anthony Bailletti speaking . . . . Mr Brown. Just a minute. [*Yelling*] Ohhhh Mister Brown. Telephone call for you. It's the premier.

[TONY *and* BROWN *change places.*

TONY *pushes with all his weight against the door, comically.*]

BROWN: Brown. . . . . Yes, Mr Premier. Yes, I saw Von Arnim this afternoon. He's a good man. . . . I agree, Mr Premier. The devices are good. They're going to work. . . . Yep. . . . Yep. . . . I told you, I'm still thinking about it. . . . No. The strike's still on for the moment. Tell you what, though. A couple more days in this place and you can have whatever you want from me. [*Long pause. He moves to cassette, turns volumes up.*] Yes sir. . . . I think you're right. Well, thanks very much, Mr Premier. Thank you. Bye.

[BROWN *puts phone down thoughtfully. Turns off cassette. Unplugs the wires. Everything looks normal.*

He checks the front door with his ear.]

TONY: Did he say anything?

BROWN: Yep. I got him.

[*He winds back cassette. Turns it on.*

Dundon's voice comes out loud.

BROWN *leaps at the machine. Turns it off. Listens for any reaction. Puts it on soft.*]

DUNDON'S VOICE: . . . . you see Von Arnim?

BROWN'S VOICE: Yes, Mr Premier. Yes, I saw Von Arnim this afternoon. He's a good man.

DUNDON'S VOICE: Damn right. I told you the machines are good, didn't I?

BROWN'S VOICE: I agree, Mr Premier. The devices are good. They're going to work.

DUNDON'S VOICE: Right. You like them?

BROWN'S VOICE: Yep.

DUNDON'S VOICE: Are you certain?

BROWN'S VOICE: Yep.

DUNDON'S VOICE: Fine. Are you going to call this damn stupid . . . . Hold on. You men on the tap. Turn it off. I want to have a private word to Mr Brown. [*Pause.*] Thank you.

BROWN'S VOICE: I told you. I'm still thinking about it.

DUNDON'S VOICE: Look, Brown, we can negotiate. Just call it —

BROWN'S VOICE: No. The strike's still on for the moment. Tell you what though. A couple more days in this place and you can have whatever you want from me.

DUNDON'S VOICE [*laughs*]: Heh. You like it up there, do you? That waterbed comes from Denmark, you know. Look, Brown, I think we can settle this now, what? You know I have a controlling interest in Donleavy Enterprises. And you know that I want them to have the Von Arnim contract. There's nothing you can *do* about that. Just for form's sake, won't you send your men back to work for just a few days. Then the press will pat me on the back and sing "For He's a Jolly Good Fellow". Then you can blow the assembly lines *up* for all I care. Hey, you still there?

BROWN'S VOICE: Yes sir.

DUNDON'S VOICE: I want this favour, Brown. And I'm willing to pay you well for it. I just need a week till after the election. What —

[*Doorbell rings.* BROWN *turns off cassette. Ejects the tape. Puts it in pocket. Puts Bob Dylan on.*]

BROWN: What?

[SUE *enters with late night meal.*]

SUE: Hello, Richard.

BROWN: Hello.

[*They kiss fervently.* TONY *looks away discreetly. As the kisses get heavier, he gets impatient. Finally he moves to tray, piles his plate full of chicken, and starts eating morosely.*

SUE *and* BROWN *disappear into bedroom.*

TONY *chomps on.*]

[*Doorbell rings.*]

TONY: What?

STUART [*from outside door*]: Hello?

[TONY *answers the door*]

TONY: Yeah?

STUART: Is Mr Brown in?

TONY: No. He tried to escape and a couple of these monkeys [*indicates* COPS *in the corridor*] shot him.

[*The* COPS *advance on* TONY *threateningly. He gives them the Italian Finger.*]

Va Fungooloh. Come in.

[STUART *enters, closing door.* TONY *goes back to his food.*]

STUART: My name's Stuart Cobble, the premier's secretary.

[*Chomp.*]
Um — May I speak to Mr Brown?
[*Groan from within bedroom.*]
TONY: No. [*(Chomp.*]
[*Silence.*]
[*Food spilling out of his mouth*]: Jesus Christ. First day out and I can't even get a bit. Just my luck. Jesus. Everybody gets it but poor old Tony. Poor old Tony. Jesus Christ. [*etc.*]
[STUART *can't quite believe this foul-mouthed drunk. He watches agog as* TONY *drains the last of a bottle of Southern Comfort, cracks another one, and swigs.*
TONY *starts choking. He mimes for* STUART *to hit him on the back.* STUART *finally gets the message and slaps him repeatedly.*]
TONY: Thanks.
STUART: You must be Mr Bailletti.
TONY: Yeah. Call me Tony.
STUART: Thank you. You must call me Stuart.
[TONY *looks at* STUART *quizzically. The look gets longer.* STUART *panics, then relaxes. Gives* TONY *a big, sweet smile.* TONY *smiles back, chews off a big hunk of chicken, then hands the rest to* STUART, *who takes a dainty bite.*]
TONY: You want a drink? [*Hands* STUART *the bottle.*]
[STUART *chokes a bit on the first swig. Smile.*
TONY, *looking at* STUART, *moves to the bedroom door.*]
TONY: Hey, Mr Brown. There's someone here to see you.
BROWN [*from bedroom*]: Be with you in a minute.
TONY: 'Kay.
[TONY *grabs a couple of glasses and a bucket of ice. Motions* STUART *to join him on the couch.* TONY *pours two drinks that overflow. Drops some ice in suavely. The glasses overflow more. Neither of them notices.*]
STUART: What are you in prison for, Tony?
TONY: Rape.
STUART: Oh.
TONY: Yeah. Some big shot's favourite nephew.
STUART: Oh.
[BROWN *enters from bedroom in new pair of white satin slacks. Grabs some chicken.*]

BROWN: Hello, Stuart.

STUART: Hello Mr Brown. I've got to see you.

BROWN: I just spoke to the premier. What?

> [STUART *gives a worried glance at* TONY. BROWN *gestures "go on".*]

STUART: It's like this, Mr Brown. I think you should accede to the premier's requests. You know, of course, about the election. It's going to mean —

BROWN: I've told him, Stuart. In one month.

STUART: But —

BROWN: Shhhhhhh.

STUART: Mr Brown, I know I shouldn't be telling you this, but the premier is really worried. I think — I think he might get — er — disagreeable.

BROWN: Thanks, Stuart. I know that must have taken a lot of courage. What's he planning?

STUART [*ashamed*]: I can't tell you, Mr Brown. I'm sorry.

BROWN: I understand.

STUART: It would be a breach of confidence.

BROWN: Yes.

STUART: I . . .

BROWN: It's all right, Stuart. We're in the middle of a war. We're just on different sides, that's all.

STUART: Yes.

> [SUE *enters from bedroom.* BROWN *notices that they look at each other strangely.*]

BROWN: Stuart. Allow me to introduce Sue. Sue, Stuart.

STUART: Hello.

SUE: Hello.

BROWN: You better go, baby. [SUE *grabs stuff up onto tray.*] See you later.

SUE: Bye. [*Exits.*]

> [BROWN *stands looking at the door. Disappointed.*]

STUART: Well, I best be off. I suppose.

TONY: Ohhh. Don't go, Stu.

STUART: I must. [*Pats briefcase.*] No rest for the wicked, eh?

BROWN: Doesn't he ever let you sleep? Come on. Have a drink with us. Tony?

> [TONY *grabs a glass, fills it, and gives it to* BROWN. *He tops the others up (to overflowing, as usual).*]

A toast. [*They stand formal.*] May the best man win.

[*They drink.*]

STUART: Another. [TONY *refills* STUART'S *glass.*] Go down, my enemies, go down.

    [*They drink.*]

TONY: I got one. [*Suddenly well-modulated voice*] To those of us that are rudely stamped and want love's majesty. Cheated of feature by dissembling nature, deformed, unfinished, sent before our time into this breathing world scarce half made up . . . . [*He falters to a halt as the others look at him in awe.*] What are you looking at! That's from fucking Shakespeare! [*They look.*] What's wrong with that? Shit!

    [TONY *grabs a bottle of Comfort and storms off into second bedroom.*

    STUART *is mortified. He looks at* BROWN, *who indicates that* TONY *should be helped out of his mood.*

    STUART *exits to second bedroom. Door closes.* BROWN, *suddenly sober, tries to open* STUART'S *briefcase. It does not open. He finds a pin and opens the lock. He fishes through the papers till he finds the ones he was looking for. He photographs them with the camera, quickly. He puts the papers back, locks the case and puts it back in same place. He examines the photos, satisfied. He then picks up the phone.*]

BROWN: Brown. Send up some more food. No. Just some toast and a couple of jars of that paté. Thanks.

    [BROWN *looks sad. He thinks deeply, actually counting off various facts and clues on his fingers. Reaches his conclusion with a shake of his head.*]

    [*The doorbell rings.*]

BROWN: Come in.

    [SUE *enters. Pause.*]

SUE: What are you looking so sad about?

    [BROWN *looks at her.*]

    Darling, what's wrong?

    [BROWN *continues looking at her.*]

    What *is* it?

BROWN: Can you write?

SUE: Of course I can write.

    [BROWN *grabs envelope from table, hands her gold pen.*]

BROWN: Write Box 349 GPO Melbourne.

    [SUE *does so.*]

SUE [*indicating the address*]: What is it?

    [*Pause.*]

BROWN: It's a journalist sympathetic to the union. I've got the goods on Dundon right here. [*Holds up cassette.*]

SUE: What goods? What are you talking about?

BROWN [*smiles*]: I forgot. You don't know, do you?
[*Pause.*]

SUE: About what?

BROWN: It's better that you don't know, darling.

SUE: Richard. I love you. I want to know. Please.

BROWN: It's pretty involved. Dundon has a company called Donleavy Enterprises controlled by front men. They make machinery. Have you heard of the Von Arnim devices?

SUE: The pollution things?

BROWN: Yes. Dundon wants his company to get the contract to build the devices.

SUE: Just a minute. Aren't they being built by prison labour?

BROWN: That was the original idea. That's what Dundon wants to happen.

SUE: But didn't you say *he* wants to build them?

BROWN: He does.

SUE: I don't understand.

BROWN: There's an election coming up. Dundon is scared that he might lose a lot of votes because of the riots and strikes in prisons. In fact, some polls have indicated that his government might lose because of those lost votes. So, he wants the Union of Convicts to agree to build the devices so he can point to his enlightened penal reform policy and his concern for both the environment *and* the voter's hip pocket because —

SUE: Because it will cost him less to have the devices built by the prisoners.

BROWN: That's right. It will cost almost nothing to build them because, of course, he doesn't want to pay the convicts, and labour costs are the most expensive item. OK. A month after the election, Dundon's government is going to pass a law requiring every car in Victoria to have a device. That's over a million cars. Are you following?

SUE: I think so.

BROWN: OK. A couple of days after the election, there's going to be some bloody riots in the prisons and, much to poor do-gooder Dundon's regret he will be forced to remove the machinery from the prisons and turn the manufacture of the Von Arnims over to private enterprise.

SUE: Why will there be riots?

BROWN: There's going to be a sudden accidental death in the Union.

SUE: Yours?

BROWN: Yep.

SUE: The bastard!

BROWN: So, reluctantly, Dundon will call for tenders, and oooooo, it just so happens that a certain Donleavy Enterprises will *just* underbid all the others and the contract will go to them. Unfortunately, the price of the devices will have risen to about three hundred bucks each, and the Victorian government will shamefacedly tell their voting public about the law requiring compulsory fitting of devices for the good of the country. And that's a contract worth . . .

SUE: Three hundred million dollars!

BROWN: Yep. Remembering, of course, that the profit margin will only be thirty per cent of that.

SUE: How did you figure all that out?

BROWN: We killers have friends in high places. [*Pause.*] Don't even think about how I got my information. You wouldn't believe it.

SUE: But you're going to stop him, aren't you, Richard? You *know* what he's planning. You won't allow him to kill you.

BROWN: Of course not. That's where you can help.

SUE: How?

[BROWN *takes a cassette and places it in the envelope, licking it shut.*]

BROWN: Post this.

SUE: Yes. Yes. What else can I do?

[BROWN *looks at her.*]

You look at me so strangely.

BROWN: Do I darling? It's because . . . . I can't talk any more. Stuart's in the next room. Goodbye.

[SUE *is hurt by the brusque dismissal.*

She moves to the door with the envelope, then rushes back and kisses him. A big embrace.

She exits, running. BROWN *stands looking at the door. He is crying a bit.*]

[STUART *enters buttoning his vest.* TONY *follows in a towel, looking grubby.*]

TONY: Hey. This guy's not bad. I think I'm in love.

BROWN: Put your clothes on, you're going back.

TONY: To *Pentridge?*

BROWN: Yep.

TONY: Oh come on, King. What's the joke?

BROWN: Get dressed.

TONY: No!

BROWN: Do what I tell you, you stupid little dago queer.

[TONY *looks at* BROWN, *shocked. He stiffens and, for the first time, seems dignified.*]

TONY: Yes, King Richard. [*Exits to second bedroom.*]

BROWN [*looking at* STUART]: Would you rather he stayed here, Stuart?

STUART: Um. . . .

BROWN: Be nice. You two could get to know each other.

[STUART *says nothing.*]

Or would you rather he got out of this place?

STUART: You know, don't you?

BROWN: Yep. [*Pause.*] Will you do me a favour?

STUART: Yes.

BROWN: Take Tony back to Pentridge in your own car. Don't let the Twenty-seven Squad or Dundon find out what you're doing till he's back in the union.

STUART: Very well.

BROWN: Listen, Stuart. One other thing. Um — Tony's always wanted to see "Les Girls" at St Kilda, you know? Could you take him there and let him watch the funny men? He won't escape.

STUART: I know that. Tony knows the score.

BROWN: Knows the score? You're sounding like him already.

STUART: Oh God. Don't say that. He talks like some reject from *The Godfather.* [*Pause.*] I'm sorry.

BROWN: For what?

STUART: For being on the wrong side.

[*Pause.*]

BROWN: Dundon's a pig, Stuart. For all his talk about turning on the lights with the Von Arnim devices, you know what he is, don't you?

STUART: Yes.

BROWN: He's finished, Stuart. Dead. Watch out for dead men.

STUART [*shaking his head*]: He's not dead, Mr Brown. The big boys are hard to kill.

BROWN: Hmmm. [*Pause.*] Leave me alone with him [*indicating* TONY] for a minute will you?

[STUART *nods. Exits through front door. Closes it.*]
[BROWN *moves to writing desk. Starts writing.*]

BROWN: Hey, paisan, you ready yet?

[TONY *enters from second bedroom suddenly.*]

I'm sorry, Tony. I really am.

TONY: Tell me, King. Did you have a reason? Did you have to say that in front of Stuart?

BROWN: I had a reason.

TONY: All right then.

BROWN [*amused*]: You're going to make a good president, Tony. [*Taps head.*] You're learning.

TONY: Thanks, King.

BROWN: OK. Stuart's going to take you to "Les Girls" on the way back. When you get there, go to the toilet.

[BROWN *has finished writing and is stuffing the real Dundon cassette in an envelope along with the photos. He talks as he stuffs them in and writes on the envelope.*]

BROWN: In the second cubicle from the end, there's a hole in the wall dead set behind the shit pot. Put this [*indicating the envelope*] in it. Got that?

TONY: Yeah. See you soon, huh?

BROWN: Yeah. Enjoy the show.

[*They embrace like lovers.* TONY *goes to the door.*]

TONY: I never knew you could write. [*Exits.*]

[BROWN *puts on Dylan tape. Sits in the armchair with a pen and writing pad on his lap. He throws them away. Swigs Southern Comfort. He looks like a King.*]

END OF ACT III

ACT IV

Several hours later. Dawn. Light very dim. A man is talking into phone, quietly.
Lights come up slowly. The man is HARRIS. *He puts down phone. He is looking at the couch. A pair of legs in white satin pants poke out from behind it.*
He looks down at the body. Kicks it viciously.
Sits on couch and lights a smoke.
DUNDON *enters with* STUART. *He closes the door, turns on the light, glances at the body, and then sits down.*
DUNDON: How was the trip?
HARRIS: OK thanks, Mr Premier.
DUNDON: What time did the plane get in?
HARRIS: One a.m. The flight back is nine thirty-five p.m.
DUNDON: Haven't been to Singapore for years. How is it?
HARRIS: Well, it seems very nice, sir.
DUNDON: Yes. It's damned lovely this time of year. I envy you, Harris. You'll have a great time.
HARRIS: I hope so.
DUNDON: Did he give you any trouble?
HARRIS: No sir. It was like he expected it.
DUNDON: Hmmm. Did he say anything?
HARRIS: Didn't really have much time. Just enough to get a good long look at my face.
DUNDON: OK. Take care of it all, will you?
HARRIS: Yes sir. The ambulance is on the way. Just normal procedure.
DUNDON [*amused*]: Normal procedure? Jesus, Harris. How often does the Twenty-seven Squad murder people?
HARRIS [*smiles*]: Only when the government tells us to, sir.
DUNDON: Don't say that again, Harris. It's not the government's fault that a prisoner is assassinated by another prisoner right in his own cell. Understand?
HARRIS: Yes sir.
　　　[SUE *enters. Looks down at the body. She is in a state of shock. She is no longer dressed in the maid's outfit, but a plush outfit.*]
DUNDON [*kissing her on the cheek*]: Janie, my pet. You best have a drink. Harris?
　　　[HARRIS *gets her a drink.*]
　　　Let's see it. [*Pause.*] Janie, may I see it?

SUE: Oh. Sorry sir. Here. [*She hands* DUNDON *the envelope.*]
[*He opens it. Kisses cassette. A letter falls out of the envelope.*]
DUNDON: What's this?
SUE: I don't know, sir. The prisoner must have slipped it in.
DUNDON [*with a wry face*]: Hmmm. Bailletti must have written it. [*Studies letter.*] My God.
[DUNDON *rushes to the cassette player. Puts on the cassette. It plays Bob Dylan. He runs the tape back and forward, turns it over. It still plays Bob Dylan.*]
Well. Well. Read that.
HARRIS [*reads*]: Dundon. The real evidence is now in the hands of a union member outside prison. We are pleased to accept your contract for the manufacture of the Von Arnim devices since we also regard the preservation of the environment as the responsibility of every citizen. We hope that our union's log of claims will finally be accepted by your government. We would also regard it as a great personal favour if a law were to be passed that would give any member of my union engaged on the project one day remission of sentence for every one day worked on the line. I best warn you that apart from your damaging phone call, I also have copies of documents relating to Donleavy Enterprises. [*Looks up.*] Dear oh dear. Damned bad form, sir, even for you. [*Resumes reading.*] Tony Bailletti will almost certainly be elected as the new president. In the meantime, he is the caretaker and has the power to negotiate with your representatives. If he stubs his toe, I want you to make sure he doesn't get blood poisoning. If his arms are broken, it might be wise to break your own in sympathy. I have a message for Sue or whatever her name is. I loved you, you bitch. I want Harris killed. That's about it. I won, Dundon you arsehole. I won. Richard Brown.
HARRIS: How about that? He even would like you to kill me if it's not too much trouble. [*He laughs.*]
[DUNDON *smiles.* SUE *looks at* HARRIS.]
SUE: Yes. How about that?
DUNDON: Yes.
[DUNDON *leaps out of his chair straight at* HARRIS, *who gets fearful.* DUNDON *pushes him aside and goes into bedroom. Closes door.*]

[*Two ambulance attendants enter with stretcher and go about their loading business.* HARRIS *relaxes.*]

HARRIS [*to* SUE]: I won, Dundon, I won. Oo oo oo. [*Laughs.*]

[STUART *has been sitting in a corner pouring glasses of Southern Comfort that overflow; then dropping ice cubes in them, then drinking them down.*]

STUART: He had no class, did he, Harris? Nothing. [*Points to brain.*] Right?

HARRIS: Right, Mr Cobble. Right.

[STUART *looks at* HARRIS *quizzically, then returns to drinking.*]

HARRIS: I have damaging phone calls. I have copies of documents. Oooo. Ooooo. oooo. We're real scared of you, Richard. We're shaking. [*Shakes.*] See?

[*The ambulance attendants have left while* HARRIS *has been talking.* DUNDON *re-enters once they are well and truly gone.* HARRIS *hands him a drink.*]

HARRIS: There you are, sir.

DUNDON: Thanks, Harris. I've got my eye on you. You're boss stuff. OK? [*Puts hands on* HARRIS'S *shoulders.*] Well, Janie. It seems you won a heart.

SUE: Yes sir. [*They look at each other.*] I think I'll go.

DUNDON: Where?

[*Pause.*]

SUE: To my home. Do you want the address?

DUNDON: No.

[SUE *exits.*]

DUNDON: Well, he was a clever man, our King Richard.

HARRIS: *Clever?* Hahaha. That's a good one, sir. Listen, I've got a few clues about who this journalist might be. I'll check it out.

DUNDON: Uh, no, Harris. Keep a low profile till the plane leaves.

HARRIS: Oh yes. It's better that way.

DUNDON: Yes. You may as well stay here. Best not to go back to your place in case you run into someone.

HARRIS: Yes sir.

DUNDON: Look, better jump into the bedroom right now. There'll be odd bods in and out of here for a few hours yet. OK? Oh. And turn on the radio in there. I think there might be something in one of the news broadcasts.

HARRIS: Yes sir. [*Exits main bedroom. Closes the door.*]

[DUNDON *and* STUART *calmly wait till they hear music coming from the room.*]

DUNDON: Is there something on your mind, Stuart?

STUART: Not really.

DUNDON: Come on. Out with it.

STUART: It just wasn't worth it. All this.

DUNDON: You're right of course. But I just can't resist beating people. I should have shot Brown right at the beginning of this Von Arnim affair. Still. [*Shrugs.*] God, he played a good game.

STUART: Yes he did.

DUNDON: Damn it, Stuart. *Tell* me what's on your mind.

STUART: Well, I don't want to make too fine a point of it, but if *I* should ever stub my toe . . . well, I trust you understand my gist.

DUNDON [*amused*]: Yes, indeed I do. We'll make a politician out of you yet, Stuart.

STUART: Thank you, Mr Premier.

DUNDON: Whom do you recommend for Harris?

STUART: Well, the Twenty-seven Squad would do it, of course, but they'd kick up a hell of a fuss.

DUNDON: Yes. Best to put out a private contract. The bastards know too much already. [*Pause.*] Stuart? I don't suppose we should get a contract out on the whole damn squad? Hmmm?

STUART: No. I don't think that's advisable.

DUNDON: No. Anyway, you can't go through life mistrusting everybody. If you can't trust a policeman, who *can* you trust? [*They laugh.*]

STUART: And Janie?

DUNDON [*reluctantly*]: Yes. We really should. [*Pause.*] Tell the contract that it must be painless and quick. She mustn't suffer, she's done a sterling job.

STUART: Ahhhh. Enrich the time to come with smooth-faced peace,

With smiling plenty and fair prosperous days.

Now civil wounds are stopped, peace lives again.

That she may long live here, God say Amen.

DUNDON: Very good, Stuart. I do believe you're cultivating a sense of humour.

STUART: Yes.

DUNDON: Better take care of the contracts immediately.

STUART: Yes sir.

[DUNDON *exits.*]

[STUART *looks around the room. Exits to main bedroom. Re-enters with a pillow.*]

HARRIS [*poking his head out*]: What's that for?

STUART: It's a souvenir.

[HARRIS *pokes his head back in. Closes the door. The radio is muted in the bedroom.*]

END

The Father We Loved on a Beach by the Sea

Stephen Sewell

*To Margaret Anne
and to my daughter Rebekah*

The Father We Loved on a Beach by the Sea was first performed at La Boite Theatre, Brisbane, on 21 July 1978, with the following cast:

DAN	Peter Stokes
MIKEY	Daryl Hewson
JOE, a labourer, father of Dan and Mikey	Paul Eperjesi
MARY, Joe's wife	Mia Retrot
GUARDS	Bill Gentle
	Malcolm Cole
CHARLEY	Malcolm Cole
FRANK	Brett Raguse
ERNIE	Bill Gentle
MAX	Graham Thomas
GEOFF	Ron May
FOREMAN	Brian Gentle
SPEAKER	David Jessop
LEAFLETER	Daryl Hewson
PAT, Joe's brother	Graham Thomas
JIMMY	Brett Raguse
BEN	David Jessop
LON	Ron May
WOMEN IN BAR	Julie Purcell
	Katharine Mahony
MEN IN BAR	Malcolm Cole
	Bill Gentle
TONY	Brian Gentle

Directed by Jeremy Ridgman

ACT I

Scene 1

A room that could be in a hotel. Two men lounging in arm-chairs, smoking. They may be guards, or perhaps they are only waiting for something. The scene is lit by a single electric globe which is either too bright or not bright enough. The atmosphere is grubby and uncomfortable. Throughout these scenes, there should be a feeling of fragility.

DAN — a man of thirty, slight paunch, thinning hair, olive complexion — is standing, uncomfortably aware of the others' presence. He is waiting, but his impatience is perhaps characteristic, i.e., he tends to restlessness. He scans a Spanish weekly, Mundo Obrero, *which he holds in his right hand, folded in two. When* MIKEY *enters, he stuffs the paper into his coat pocket. He is wearing an out-of-fashion overcoat on top of a well-worn conservative suit, with a white shirt open at the neck. His voice is strong and vibrant, if perhaps a little gravelly. He is accustomed to public speaking, and is a good orator.*

MIKEY, *whose entrance marks the beginning of dialogue, is six years younger, and has a raw, blunt manner. He is wearing a pullover and light-coloured corduroy pants. The uncertainty of adolescence still clings to him, but is tinged with an assurance which oscillates between arrogance and common sense. He is carrying an umbrella.*

At the beginning of the scene, there is a long period of relative inactivity. In fact, throughout the play, the importance of pauses and silences cannot be overstated.

The sound of light rain is heard. After a short time, an argument becomes audible somewhere far off. It remains irritatingly indistinct.

There is a knock at the door. DAN *walks quickly across, and opens it. The first two lines — as* DAN *and* MIKEY *are greeting each other — are spoken more or less simultaneously. They shake hands, etc.*

DAN: G'day! How you been keepin'?

MIKEY: How you goin'!

DAN: Geez, ay, look at this [*indicating the umbrella*]. A living example of the innate respectability of the working class.

Where's Peter? I thought he'd be with you.

MIKEY: Isn't he here? What time is it?

DAN: Just after half past.

MIKEY: Maybe he's gettin' some piss.

DAN: Peter! He's joined the legion, has he? You're looking pretty healthy. Still working?

MIKEY: Yeah. Dunno how long for but. They put off a couple o' blokes last week. What about you?

DAN: Me? Yeah, yeah. Come hail and shit the juggernaut of revolution forges on. You want a drink?

MIKEY: Oh yeah. Whaddaya got?

DAN: Smirnoff Vodka, served at the tables of the Czars, 1813 to 1917.

MIKEY: No beer, ay?

DAN: Come on, mate, you want to put hairs on your chest, don't you?

MIKEY: Yeah, all right.

[*The conversation continues while* DAN *looks about for his travelling bag.*]

DAN: So what's been happening?

MIKEY: Nothin' much. Have you got any chairs?

DAN: Ay? Oh, yeah, over the side there.

[*He indicates two kitchen chairs, which* MIKEY *brings forward.*]

What's Peter doing?

MIKEY: Yeah, he's all right. Did you know we got a house together.

DAN: No. [*Sights his travelling bag.*] Oh, here it is. What'd I put it there for? When that happen? [*He opens the bag and extracts the bottle — a flask — while* MIKEY *answers.*]

MIKEY: Oh, the old man was gettin' on me nerves, and Pete was lookin' for somewhere to live so we decided to get a place together.

DAN: Here you go. [*He hands the bottle to* MIKEY.]

MIKEY: What about a glass?

DAN: Jesus Christ McCloud! You think I'm gonna disease you?

[MIKEY *shrugs and takes an experimental sip.*]

MIKEY: Geez! What do you drink that stuff for?

DAN: History, comrade. Cheers!

[DAN *takes a large gulp and hands the bottle back.*]

MIKEY: No. I don't want any more.

DAN: Go on! It'll warm you up.

[MIKEY *takes the bottle reluctantly.*]
So what's it like?

MIKEY: What?

DAN: The new house.

MIKEY: Oh, it's all right.

DAN: You don't sound too enthusiastic.

MIKEY: Yeah. Oh, we're gettin' on each other's nerves, I s'pose. I'm lookin' to stay at some place else. You still workin' for the coms?

DAN: You call what I do work? A slave has an easier time.

MIKEY: How long you down for?

DAN: I'll be leaving tomorrow.

MIKEY: Where for?

DAN: I don't know. Depends on what happens tonight. How's your girl?

MIKEY: Ay? Oh, I give her the arse. She was always hangin' round, you know. Couldn't go anywhere without her wantin' to come along. Give you the shits.

DAN: You just gonna hang onto it, are you?

MIKEY: Ay? Yeah, all right.
[*He takes another tentative sip and hands the bottle back.*]

DAN: Yeah, you were saying about Peter?

MIKEY: Oh, I dunno. Nothin' much has happened.

DAN: He still thinking about becoming a priest?

MIKEY: No, I think he give that one up. He's been talkin' about doin' some work with alcoholics. Went for an interview the other day. Dunno how he did but. Never talks to you much. You still livin' at the same place?

DAN: Which place was that?

MIKEY: The one you were at last time.

DAN: Oh, no. No, I've moved a couple o' times since then.

MIKEY: Don't it give you the shits movin' round like that?

DAN: I don't know. Sometimes.
[*Pause.*]

MIKEY: I read they got Ramon Gris the other day.

DAN: Yeah. [*Pause.*] How's the old man?

MIKEY: He's fucked.
[*Blackout: simultaneously,* JOE — *who has been watching the whole scene* — *is spotlit. He is dressed in baggy, striped pyjamas. He is left staring ahead sufficiently long for the*

atmosphere of angry helplessness to be communicated.
Scene 2 begins properly with MARY'S *first line, when the*
lights are gradually brought up on the whole scene.]

Scene 2

The kitchen of a suburban house. As in the previous scene, the
perspective is somehow wrong. The wall — a flat — is too high. A
large wooden table with a single chair is positioned at an angle to
the wall. There is a feeling of griminess — the wall, though not
dirty, is greasy above the level one can reach with an arm — the
stove is hidden behind another flat, a sort of partition wall. MARY
is wearing a dressing gown and slippers.
    The sound of light rain, which was used throughout the
previous scene, was faded out during the interval with JOE.
    MARY'S *first words signal the steady increase in lights.*
    JOE *is thirty-three,* MARY *is twenty-nine.*
MARY: Joe? . . . Joe? What's wrong?
    [JOE *turns and faces her. Long pause. She comes closer.*]
    What's wrong, love?
JOE: Where are the kids?
MARY: They're in bed asleep. Why? What's the matter, love?
    [*Pause.*]
JOE: I don't know . . . I can't sleep.
MARY: What time is it? Must be nearly three o'clock . . . Come to
    bed.
    [*She puts her arm around his waist and draws him toward*
    the door. At first he complies, but then he stops.]
JOE: I'll get a job tomorrow.
MARY: Come to bed. It's too late.
JOE: No . . . No, I mean it . . . . I feel lucky. . . . . I'll get a job down
    the Commonwealth . . . .
MARY: Let's go to bed. It's hours yet.
JOE: I can't sleep.
MARY: Do you want a glass of milk?
JOE: If I get there early enough . . . I'll go now, ay?

MARY: You can't go now. It's too early. Nobody'll be there.
JOE: What's the time? Turn on the radio, will you?
MARY: It'll wake the kids.
    [*He gets up to leave.*]

MARY: What are you doing?

JOE: I'll just go and get dressed.

MARY: Joe! It's three in the morning. Nobody'll be there for hours yet.

JOE: But you got to be there first. See, that's the problem .... I'm never first. If I go now it'll be all right.

MARY: But you don't even know they've got a job!

JOE [*sharply*]: They'll have a job!

MARY: Why will they?

JOE: Because they're a big place, that's why.

MARY: They've been laying off like all the rest of 'em.

[*Pause.*]

JOE [*angrily*]: There's got to be somethin'! I just haven't tried hard enough. But it's gonna be different, I can just feel it. I'll — I'll — I'll get a job tomorrow, I know.

MARY: Why not at least wait till the newsagent opens?

JOE: Yeah, yeah. That's a good idea. I'll do that. Can't be too tired on the first day. Wouldn't want to get the sack on the first day ... It's gonna be good again, I can just feel it .... We'll do this thing right. ... Yeah, boy .... I'll — I'll — I'm not gonna take no for an answer. ... You ironed me shirt, didn't you.

MARY: What's wrong, Joe?

JOE: There's nothin' wrong! I'm gonna get a job. Doesn't that make you happy?

MARY: There's no use building up your hopes.

JOE: It's not a hope! I just need a bit more confidence, that's all. You got to believe in what you want. You got to make it happen.

MARY: All right. All right. Have it your way.

JOE: I'll have a bath an' ... an' then I'll put on me shirt .... They'll gimme a job for sure .... It's gonna be all right .... Don't you think I will!

MARY: Keep your voice down, you want to wake the kids!

JOE: Where's Dan?

MARY: I told you. He's in bed asleep.

[*Pause.*]

JOE: It's like a dream.

[JOE *stands and moves forward. Lights down on* MARY. JOE *slowly spotlit.*]

Scene 3

As at the end of scene 1, JOE *spotlit. The set remains the same, as it is returned to in scene 4.* MARY *remains motionless. Everything blacked out except* JOE.

JOE: Excuse me, mister ... I was lookin' for some work... I wonder... [*He realizes he is still wearing pyjamas.*] Where are me clothes?... What am I doin' without me clothes?... Oh, geez. Look, mister, I'll do anything.... I been out of work, you know... three months... tried everything. No one's puttin' on. I — I — I — don't want to waste your time ... I'll do anything ... Haven't got nothin', ay? Oh well, s'pose I'll try some place else.... Thanks for your time ....

[*Pause.*]

Jesus Christ! What's a man supposed to do! What can you do, ay? What can you fuckin' do! Grovel like a gutless worm on the fuckin' floor! Jesus help me ....

[*Pause.*]

I'm not a bludger. I had a job. I'll tell you .... There was the electrolytic place in Lidcombe — that's where I got me dermatitis. Acid, you know... an' then I worked at Clyde Engineering. Oh boy, that was a good job... Good.... In the war — I never told you, did I — I didn't become a soldier. Knew blokes that did. I didn't want to get killed. [*Laughs.*]... No, so see I got this doctor to give me a certificate like.... I was workin' in the AWA place along Parramatta Road — or was that later? Oh, I can't remember. Doesn't matter — that's when I started goin' with your mother... She was in the lolly place, that's right.... Yeah, that was a good job.... I worked.... I been workin' all me life . I was gonna be a farmer, you know. You can live off the land. Even when there's no money, you can catch rabbits to eat, like me brother Harry done .... You remember him, don't you .... Harry .... All you have to do is work an' save up your money. When you got enough, you can buy some land. They sell it for a song out west... hundreds of acres for a bob each. Run some sheep on it. Get bees, and a few horses to ride. Have a cow — make your own cheese an' butter. Live off the fat of the land. No one tellin' you what to do. Joe do this. Joe do that. Joe you were in the toilet too long. Joe pick up your pay.

Nothin' like that. Out there you're free. Free as the ... free as the wind. If it's rainin' you can spend the day in bed. Milk the cow first. Got to milk the cow, otherwise it'll get sick and you got to get another one. Yeah, yeah, milk the cow first, and collect the eggs. Oh boy, fresh eggs. We're gonna have a couple o' dozen chooks. Don't have to feed 'em. They just scratch around by 'emselves. Knock their heads off for Sunday dinner — you ... you wouldn't have to do that ... I'd do that meself .... Roast chicken and baked potatoes, with peas straight from the garden. Yeah, and a bit o' butter — not too much, bad for the heart — just a bit meltin' over the hot potatoes. And there's no school out there ... you wouldn't have to go to school no more. I never liked it either. ... We'll have a good time. All of us together again .... If we just save up the money ... Jesus help me! What'd I do! What'd I ever do! ... I'll — I'll get a job .... I haven't tried hard enough, that's what it is .... I'll get a job in the mornin' and then we can start plannin' ... If we save a couple o' quid a week that's ... that's a hundred and four pounds in a year. We could save two quid easy, maybe even a bit more ... and then there's the interest .... Put it in the bank. A nest egg. One hundred and four pounds. We could get somethin' .... Don't you see.

[*Throughout the latter part of this scene,* MARY *has been crying, her sobs growing slowly audible. At the end, lights up.*]

Scene 4

Setting as in scene 3. Mary crying.

JOE: What's wrong with my little girl?

MARY: Joe?

JOE: Hey, geez ... what's the matter?

[*Pause. She wipes her face.*]

MARY: I'm frightened. Something awful is happening to us. What's wrong?

JOE: There's nothin' wrong .... Listen, Mary, I was just thinkin' .... We got to get out of the city .... It's no place to raise kids .... What do you reckon we buy a farm?

MARY: How could we buy a farm?

JOE: I don't mean now. I mean when we get back on our feet. I
     figured it out. We could save a hundred 'n four pounds just
     in a year. I could get a couple o' jobs even. Get one under a
     different name so they don't find out. Wouldn't even take a
     year.

MARY: Where do you get these ideas from? What could we do on a
     farm? You don't know the first thing about farmin'.

JOE: [*angrily*]: I could learn .... I'll read some books an' find
     out. Anyhow, country people are real friendly. They'd show
     us. It won't be hard. Just got to work, that's all. Wouldn't
     you like it out in the bush? We'll have our own cow and a
     couple o' horses for the kids. You can make butter ....
     Wouldn't you like it? What's the matter.

MARY: It won't work, Joe.

JOE: It will! I'll make it work ... I'll read up ... I'll find out ...
     It'll be good. It's just a rat race. It'll — It'll —

MARY: But what about the kids' school?

JOE: They don't need school. Just teach 'em a lot of garbage.
     Never teach 'em the real stuff like where the food comes
     from or anything like that. I never went to school.

MARY: And look what you are now. Wake up, Joe. You want them
     to go through the same things? Always scrimpin' and savin'
     so there's enough to eat. They got to have an education.

JOE [*scornfully*]: Education. What for? So they can sit in an
     office the rest of their lives? We got to get out. We got to give
     'em somethin' better. Out there, it's different.

MARY: It's not. It's all the same. Farmers are goin' broke just like
     everyone else. I heard it on the radio. Can't even get
     anybody to buy the land, so they just walk off it. Hundreds
     of 'em just walkin' off to look for work in the city.

JOE: They're not!

MARY: I heard it, I tell you.

JOE: Maybe some of 'em ... but look at the big cars they drive. I
     never heard a farmer goin' broke. They wouldn't walk off.

MARY: I heard it.

JOE: Well, you musta heard wrong.

MARY: All right, call me a liar.

JOE: Maybe it was somewhere else they was talkin' about.

MARY: It wasn't! It was here in New South Wales, and it's the
     same all over. Queensland the same. And Victoria. No one's
     got any money. It's a depression, Joe.

JOE: It'll get better. They wouldn't let it happen again. Got better last time, didn't it? It's not a depression at all. They wouldn't let it happen again.

MARY: Well, there's no money on the land, anyhow.

JOE: Why do you have to be like this? Why can't you see it my way sometimes? Don't you think I want it for you, too?

MARY: We'd starve on the land.

JOE: We wouldn't. I've got me gun.

MARY: That'd be nice, wouldn't it. Livin' on rabbit the rest of our lives.

JOE: It'd only be like that for a while. Till we got on our feet. Then we wouldn't have any worries.

[*Pause.*]

MARY: Can't we talk about it in the morning?

JOE: No.

[*Pause.*]

MARY: So what're you gonna do?

JOE: First thing, I'll — I'll get a job. I'll get one in the mornin', and then we'll save up some money — we'll have to make a budget and stick to it. No extra expenses — put the money in the bank soon as I get paid. Then . . . . then I'll get the paper and we can find a place out west somewhere. Then when I got the money we can go.

MARY: It's gonna take a lot more than a hundred and four pounds, I can tell you that now.

JOE: Why? Jesus, that's a lot of money.

MARY: What about food when we get there? And petrol. And we'll have to take clothes and tools. You just can't buy the land and leave it at that.

[*Pause.*]

JOE: Well, we'll . . . it might take a bit longer.

MARY: And what about a doctor. You can't go out in the middle of the bush with your health the way it is.

JOE: Why can't you help me for once! Why do you always have to be like this when I want to do somethin'!

MARY: Because we got three kids to look after, that's why. Go off half cocked on some hair-brained idea. You just can't go off like that. It's different now. You're not single any more.

JOE: Jesus, sometimes I wish I was.

[*Pause.*]

MARY: Neither of us are.

[*Pause.*]

JOE: It could've been good.

MARY: It wouldn't be much good if we starved to death.

JOE: I'm a good husband, ain't I? I only want the best for you, you know that, don't you?

MARY: Yes. [*Pause.*] Things'll get better, you wait an' see. I've been prayin' to Our Lord. He'll look after us. He won't let anything happen to us.

JOE: I'm frightened, Mary . . . The whole world's gone mad. Every time you pick up the paper, somethin' terrible's happened . . . . Mary . . . do you reckon the communists are gonna come?

MARY: I don't know.

JOE: I wouldn't let 'em take you.

MARY: We'll be all right.

JOE: I'd shoot you rather than let that happen.

MARY: Joe!

[*Blackout.*]

Scene 5

The gates of Commonwealth Engineering. A group of between ten and fifteen men standing about waiting for work. It's a cold morning, Tuesday 27 April 1959. Barely light. Men dressed shabbily in a wide range of cheap but warm clothing. Overcoats, pullovers, and beanies seem to predominate, with yellow, green, and grey being the main colours. Scene lit by a street light. Some stand alone, others stand in groups.

CHARLEY: There was only fifty thousand in forty-six. Biggest fuckin' Anzac Day in thirteen years. What do you reckon, ay? Biggest fuckin' Anzac Day in thirteen years.

FRANK: Yeah, heard it on the radio.

CHARLEY: Shoulda come down. Ain't nothin' like marchin' down the street, everyone cheerin'. All the boys were there, even some of the old codgers from the Boer War. And then there was the young blokes from Malaya. By geez, didn't they look good too. No fuckin' worries with young blokes like that wearin' the uniform.

FRANK: You reckon the Yanks'll be doin' anything 'bout that Cuba place?

CHARLEY: Fuckin' oath. Can't have bloody coms on your doorstep, can you. Be just like if they was in New Guinea, wouldn't it. Stands to reason.

FRANK: Yeah, I s'pose.

CHARLEY: They're fanatics, that's the problem with them reds. Fuckin' fanatics, that's what they are. Like ants. Can't stop 'em till the last one's dead. Just the same as the Japs. Somethin' wrong with the cunts . . . .

[*As* CHARLEY *is speaking,* JOE *enters wearing an overcoat similar to the one worn by* DAN *in scene 1. A Sydney Morning Herald is sticking out of his pocket. He does not know anybody.*]

. . . Shoulda fuckin' dropped the bomb on 'em. No good just killin' the soldiers. Fuckin' cunts breed like rabbits. It's just like Lang said. It's them or us. A fuckin' white world or a fuckin' yellow one. No good foolin' round with the cunts. Drop the fuckin' bomb on 'em . . . . What do you reckon, Ernie?

ERNIE: Ay?

CHARLEY: What do you reckon 'bout them reds. Kill the fuckin' lot, ay? That's what I reckon.

ERNIE: What's wrong with you? Wouldn't the old lady give you a root last night?

MAX: Musta hit the piss yest'y, ay Ernie?

CHARLEY: S'pose you went to church, did you?

ERNIE: Me and Max spent the day in prayer and meditation, didn't we mate?

MAX: Like altar boys.

FRANK: Prayin' for more piss, I bet.

CHARLEY: Prayin' for that mutt of his, more likely. What'd it come last Friday, Ernie? Ran into the fence, didn't it?

[GEOFF *walks on-stage. Approaches* JOE.]

GEOFF: G'day Joe, how you goin'?

JOE: Oh, g'day Geoff . . . real good, real good. How 'bout yourself?

GEOFF: Not bad. Reckon they'll put this crew on?

JOE: Oh, I dunno. Few of 'em here, ain't there.

GEOFF: Same everywhere you go.

JOE: Yeah . . . . Things don't look too good.

GEOFF: Got to get better sooner or later.

JOE: Yeah, I was thinkin' that meself. Can't go on like this, can it?

GEOFF: Not if Menzies wants to stay in, that's for sure.

JOE: No . . . no. . . . He's gonna have to do something. Can't let it go on, can he? . . . I — I don't think Evatt'd be much better though, do you?

GEOFF: They're all politicians, aren't they.

JOE: Yeah. I think if Evatt got in, the unions'd have too much power.

GEOFF: Yeah. What's the time, Joe?

[JOE *looks quickly at his watch.*]

JOE: Quarter to seven.

GEOFF: Won't be much longer then. How you managin'?

JOE: Just hangin' on. We had a bit saved, so it hasn't been as bad as it might have. What about yourself?

GEOFF: We're OK. Been able to get a couple of odd jobs. Mowin' lawns, that sort of thing.

JOE: You been mowin' lawns?

GEOFF: Yeah. Handyman stuff, you know. Fixin' broken windows, bit of paintin'. Enough to keep me busy and make a bit on the side.

JOE: Yeah, it's a bugger, ain't it, not havin' anything to do. Enough to drive you round the bend. . . . I been doin' a few things round the house meself. . . . How do you get your jobs?

GEOFF: Just watch the casual employment section. Always got something. Been able to make a quid a day.

JOE: You don't say. Gee . . . I — I hadn't even thought of that.

GEOFF: Got to keep your eyes open.

JOE: Yeah. Geez ay . . . casual employment section, you say. . . . I'll — I'll remember that. That's a real good idea, Geoff. I'll do that.

GEOFF: No good sittin' round the house doin' nothin'. No tellin' how long you'll be off.

JOE: That's right . . . . I — I haven't — I been doin' a few things, you know. Spend a lot of time on the car and that sort of thing.

GEOFF: Havin' trouble with it?

JOE [*laughs*]: Bugger of a thing. Have to work on it all the time to keep it goin'. It's too old, that's the thing. Must be at least fifteen years old now.

GEOFF: Don't last forever, do they?

JOE [*laughs*]: No, don't last forever, that's for sure. Be good if they did but, wouldn't it?

GEOFF: You got to have a car.

[*Pause.*]

[*Two men enter, dressed like the others. One is carrying an orange crate, which he puts down. The other distributes leaflets.*]

GEOFF: Wonder what this is?

CHARLEY [*loudly*]: What's this then? [*Reads*] The working man starves while the bosses sip champagne. Fuckin' commo shit. [*To the leafleter*] Why don't you go back to Moscow where you belong, you fuckin' red traitor.

LEAFLETER: Stick it up your arse.

CHARLEY: I'll show you, you fuckin' commo rat!

FIRST MAN [*standing on the crate*]: Comrades! Why fight amongst ourselves when it's the bosses we should be fighting.

FRANK: Go back to Russia!

FIRST MAN: Why isn't there any work? Do you think it's your fault! Or do you think maybe it's an act of God like a rainy day?

CHARLEY: We don't want to hear this bullshit!

FIRST MAN: I'll tell you why. It's because the bosses don't give a stuff about you or your families. All they care about is how much money you can make 'em. All they care about is exploiting the working class!

JOE: It's not true! Don't listen to him, boys.

FIRST MAN: Open your eyes, mates. Where did the jobs go? A year ago they couldn't get enough of yous to sweat in the factories. They had to bring 'em out from Italy and Greece, they were goin' so hard. And what happened? They over-produced. They made so many things that nobody wanted 'em . . .

JOE: It's the union's fault, they're too greedy.

FIRST MAN: So what do they do? Carry the workers on the profits they'd made out of us? You'd have to be jokin'. Throw the workers in the rubbish. Turf 'em out. They'll still be there when we need 'em. That's what the bosses are sayin'. You know what they think of yous? You wanna know what they think you are? Bludgers. You're lazy and you smell. You're good for nothin' but shit work, because that's what you are, the shit of the earth. And if you reckon they don't, start readin' the editorials in them *Sydney Mornin' Heralds* yous have all got stuffed in your pockets. You're dead men, because you have to work with your hands to make a livin' . . . .

CHARLEY: Fuckin' commo rat.

FIRST MAN: Who built this factory? Workers did. Who makes the products? Workers do. Who builds the roads? Who mans the ships? Who produces the wealth? Workers, that's who.

But who gets the profits? The bosses. They get rich and we
get fuck all . . . .

CHARLEY: It's a fuckin' lie!

FIRST MAN: Why won't you open your bloody eyes!

CHARLEY: I know what's goin' on. I fought in the fuckin' war.

FIRST MAN: What did you fight for? Freedom, was that it? What
sort of freedom have you got? The freedom to starve. That's
what it is under capitalism. The freedom to exploit the
working man. What do you think Menzies is doin' while
you're out here scroungin' for a job? You think he gives a
stuff? You know what his solution to capitalist inflation is?
You bein' out of a job, that's what it is. Keep the working
class in their place. Give 'em a dose of bein' on the dole to
show 'em how lucky they are to work in a hellhole half the
day. That's what I come to tell you, mates. Pig-iron Bob
Menzies leaves on a world tour with Dame Pattie
tomorrow. Two months he's takin' off, because he's a tired
man. That's what he thinks of you lot. You can all go to
hell. You and your families both, but Pig-iron's takin' a
holiday. [*To Charley*] You ought to remember how he got
named Pig-iron. It was the pig-iron he wanted to sell to the
Japs that woulda killed your mates if the workers hadn't
stopped him. The worker's mate, not the boss's. They wasn't
the ones who was gonna get shot. The war was the best
thing that ever happened to 'em. While we were gettin'
slaughtered, they were stashin' the money away in Swiss
banks. And can you remember what Menzies had to say
'bout Hitler before the war, ay? Hitler's a good bloke,
reckons old Bob. Hitler's killin' the coms, so he must be a
good bloke. That's what he thinks of the working class,
that's what he thinks of us. If they step out of line, shoot
'em. And you reckon we won the war against fascism. The
workers have got to stick together. There's a demonstration
tomorrow at Martin Place, and any one of yous that doesn't
show deserves the kick in the guts he gets when the boss
decides there's no work. Look at yourselves. Is there a man
amongst you? Standin' round like a mob of sheep hopin' to
get the chopper before one of the other mugs does. Hey,
mister, can you give us a job? We've got to fight for our
rights. We don't owe the bosses the time of day. This is our
country, built on the blood and sweat of the working class.
Sack the bosses, comrades. Show 'em you've still got some

dignity left. Demonstrate tomorrow and march on May Day . . . .

[*The Commonwealth Engineering gate rattles open and the men immediately turn to the foreman who steps out.*]

FOREMAN: What are you doing here? Piss off before I call the cops. Go on, fuck off! [*To the others*] We need one bloke. [*Looks around and selects the biggest.*] You'll do. [*He turns to go back inside.*]

CHARLEY: You gonna need any more?

FOREMAN: Come back in the morning.

FIRST MAN: Come back in the morning.

[FOREMAN *and worker disappear behind the gate. Men begin to drift off.*]

CHARLEY: What are you gonna do?

FRANK: Fucked if I know.

CHARLEY: What time is it?

FRANK: Seven.

CHARLEY: Want to go down the early opener?

FRANK: Might as well. Nothin' else to fuckin' do.

CHARLEY: You want to come, Ern?

ERNIE: No. I might try somewhere else.

CHARLEY: If they're not puttin' on here, they won't be puttin' on anywhere, mate.

ERNIE: Might be lucky.

CHARLEY: Suit yourself. What about you, Max?

MAX: Might come down for a couple.

CHARLEY: OK, see you later, Ernie. You'll know where we are.

ERNIE: Yeah, see you later.

[*They leave.* JOE *and* GEOFF *still on.*]

GEOFF [*heatedly*]: They're all the same. Never tell you what it's like in Russia but, do they?

JOE: There ought to be a law to stop 'em. Somethin's got to happen, don't it? Can't go on like this.

GEOFF: Well, I've got me gun.

JOE: They want to destroy the country. I don't reckon he fought in the war, do you?

GEOFF: He didn't say which side, did he? I can remember. Bloody signed a peace treaty with Hitler when they were gassin' the Jews. Listen to him you'd think they won the bloody war. No better than the Nazis. Twist things around till you believe black is white. Bloody coms. It's their fault things are as bad as they are. Always strikin' for more money. Should all be locked up.

JOE: I dunno what's gonna happen.

GEOFF: It's gonna come to a fight, that's what's gonna happen. Bastards.

[*Pause.*]

GEOFF: I'm goin'. See you later.

JOE: Yeah, all right Geoff. Look after yourself.

[GEOFF *leaves.* JOE *looks about, and then goes off in another direction. Fadeout.*]

Scene 6

As in scene 1 except that one of the men is missing, and DAN *is sitting restlessly in the armchair he had occupied. He appears slightly feverish. There is a certain amount of self-parody in his manner. The sound of light rain, as before.*

DAN: Remember how he used to say it when we were kids: "The Communists are destroyin' the country." Jesus Christ, he spent his whole fucking life copping shit in the factories and that was the sum total of his contribution to human understanding. The fucking Communists. I can remember dragging along behind him when he was out of work. One fucking factory after another. "Oh boy, this looks like a good place." But then, after a while he'd come out looking like he'd been whipped. "Better try some place else, ay?" There wasn't a trace of self-respect left in his body. They beat it out of him. Not the Communists, but the fucking bosses.

[*Pause.*]

MIKEY: You heard from Kate?

DAN: No. No, she wouldn't be able to find me even if she wanted.

[*Pause.*]

MIKEY: How old would Sarah be now?

DAN: Ay? Oh, five I think. Five in June.

[*Pause.*]

MIKEY: You miss 'em?

DAN [*sharply*]: What difference would it make? [*Pause.*] I'm sorry, Mike. I've got a few things on my mind. [*Laughs.*] The monsters are loose, master. [*Pause.*] Did you ever meet Rhonda?

MIKEY: No, I don't think so.
[*Pause.*]

DAN: Oh — we lived together for a couple of years. [*Pause.*]
Before the dictatorship. She was a journalist, you know.
They picked her up the first day and kept her locked up for
a week. She was able to get a visa to Italy.
[*Pause.*]

MIKEY: Yeah. I didn't even know about it till the shop steward
come around an' told us. It was real funny — you know —
couple of the blokes reckoned we should go out on strike.
[*Laughs.*]

DAN: What'd the rest think?
[*Pause.*]

MIKEY: Oh, everyone was real confused, I s'pose. No one knew
what to do. Didn't seem real. This little Hungarian bloke
was jumpin' up an' down sayin' we should all go home an'
get our guns to defend democracy. [*Laughs.*] Yeah, I
dunno. Still doesn't seem real to me — like it's not sort of as
bad as what you'd think, don't you reckon?

DAN: Anyone you know get arrested?

MIKEY: Just the shop steward, but he was a bastard anyway —
never did nothin' but collect the bloody dues. [*Laughs.*]
Wanted to be foreman, you know. [*Pause.*] What about
you?

DAN: Yeah, I knew a few.
[*Pause.*]

MIKEY: Oh, I think people take things too seriously. There's
always gonna be a boss, isn't there.

DAN: What're you fucking talking about? There were five
thousand arrests in Sydney that Amnesty International
knows about. A thousand of them are already dead and the
rest are still in jail. Every day they find another body
somewhere — like that woman wrapped in barbed wire on
Manly beach the other day. You know how they figured out
it was a woman? There was a tit floating in the surf. Jesus
Christ — is that something you can take lightly? [*Pause.*]
Fuckin' hell, that's the sort of attitude that's landed us
where we are. [*Pause.*] What would you do if you got
arrested going home tonight because you're my brother?
Put it down to experience? Have a laugh with the cops?
Fuck me. [*Pause.*] I don't have a name any more — none
of us do — because when you've got a name, your family

can be traced. Do you understand what I'm saying? That's the sort of fucking world we're living in now.

MIKEY: Yeah, all right. [*Pause.*] You want a smoke?

DAN: No. Bad for your health. [*Laughs.*] Jesus Christ, it's hot in here.
[*He opens one of the windows. The sound of a car cruising down the wet street. An insipid breeze brushes the curtains.* MIKEY *lights a cigarette. Pause.*]

DAN: Where's the booze?

MIKEY: Haven't you got it?

DAN: Have I? Oh, yeah. Here's mud in your eye. [*He takes a gulp.*] Dad no good, you reckon.

MIKEY: No. [*Pause.*] He let himself go. Just eatin' out o' tins an' stuff like that.

DAN: S'pose he's hittin' the piss, is he?

MIKEY: Yeah. Never sees anyone. [*Pause.*] He's been no good since Mum died.
[*Pause.*]

DAN: You see him much?

MIKEY: No. I go around sometimes, but it's always the same. Won't talk to you. You know how he used to be. [*Pause.*] You gonna go an' see him?
[*Pause.*]

DAN: I don't know. Maybe.
[*Blackout.*]

Scene 7

JOE *and* MARY. *A spare set. Perhaps only the kitchen table.* JOE *seated.* MARY *standing, shelling peas into a saucepan.* JOE *is wearing pyjamas and a ratty dressing-gown.* MARY *wears a cotton print frock.*
The intermittent sound of cars is heard, with the occasional sound of a lorry labouring in low gear: there is a highway nearby.
Pause after lights up.

MARY: Quiet, isn't it.
[*Pause.*]

JOE: Where are the kids?

MARY: Off down the street somewhere.

JOE: They're gettin' big, aren't they.

MARY: Yes. They're growin' up fast.

JOE: Do you reckon any of 'em are like me?

MARY: Barb reckoned Dan's like you.

JOE: Did she?

MARY: Yeah. Same nose, she said. Does look a bit like you, too.

JOE: Wonder what they'll be like when they grow up.

MARY: S'pose they'll have their own worries.

JOE: Why can't life be simple?

MARY: Makes you wonder, don't it.

JOE: Nothin' seems to make sense any more. It wasn't always like that, was it?

MARY: I don't know. S'pose people've always had their troubles.
[*Pause.*]

JOE: I get frightened sometimes thinkin' about it.

MARY: Nothin' much we can do.
[*Pause.*]

JOE: I saw Geoff today.

MARY: Did you? How was he?

JOE: Good.

MARY: Why don't you ever go an' see him any more? You used to be good mates.

JOE: I dunno. [*Pause.*] It's funny how things change, isn't it. [*Pause.*] How long will tea be?

MARY: Half an hour. Why don't you put on the radio?
[*He does so mechanically. Pause.*]

JOE [*suddenly*]: Why does it always have to be like this?

MARY: What?

JOE: Oh, sittin' around the house all night. Let's go for a drive, ay?

MARY: The kids'll want their tea in a little while. We can go for a drive tomorrow, that'd be nice.

JOE: I want to go now. I want to get out, do something.

MARY: Can't go now. If you'd've told me earlier we could've gone to the pictures or something.
[*Pause.*]

JOE: I don't know what to do.

MARY: Sweep the floor if you want something to do. Just look around you. There's plenty of things to do.
[*Pause. She embraces him.*]
Cheer up, love.

JOE: You wouldn't leave me, would you Mary?

MARY: Course not. We're married, aren't we? What put that silly thought into your head?

JOE: I dunno. Things are gettin' me down. Sometimes I think the

whole world's gone mad. [*Pause.*] Look at that place
Cuba. They been doin' some terrible things there. I was
readin' in the paper how they was killin' people. Women an'
little kids. Just slittin' their throats — all sorts of horrible
things. An' how they're startin' in some other places.
Vietnam or some place, it's called. Up there somewhere. It's
like a disease.

MARY: We can only pray that things'll work themselves out.

JOE: It just seems like it's comin' to the end. It's even happenin'
here. Communists in the unions — there was even one down
the Commonwealth Engineering this mornin' tryin' to
cause trouble. Why don't people understand, Mary? We got
to fight it before it gets a grip on the country.
[*Pause.*]

MARY: I don't know. You just do what you can, I s'pose. No use
worryin' about it.

JOE: There's got to be somethin' we can do. It can't go on like it
has been.

MARY: We're only little people, love.
[*Pause.*]

JOE: Little people. Little people with little mean lives and kids
that grow up to hate 'em.

MARY: Joe! That's not true. Why do you say that?
[*Pause.*]

JOE: I'm gonna be a better man for you, Mary, I promise you. I'll
make you happy. And I'll be a good father. We'll all go
fishin' together or somethin', ay?

MARY: That'd be a turn-up.

JOE: Yeah, we'll do things together. We'll all be mates again. We
got to stick together, that's the thing. Don't you see?

MARY: But we are together, Joe.

JOE: But we got to stay closer, look after each other. Don't you
see, Mary? They're tryin' to kill us.

MARY: Who?

JOE: The Russians.

MARY: Oh, don't be silly. Why do you think that?

JOE: Read it in the papers every day. It's just like Billy Graham
was sayin' the other day. It's the prophecy. Wars an'
rumours of wars. Earthquakes an' starvation. It's
happenin' now.

MARY: Them blokes are always predictin' the end. They don't

know what they're talkin' about. If you listened to them you wouldn't be able to sleep at night.

JOE: This time it's true.

MARY: Why is it?

JOE: Because you can see it with your own bloody eyes, that's why.

[*Pause.*]

MARY: Even if it is, what can you do?

JOE: See it every day. The Communist're takin' over the country. All them strikes, they're just to make us weak so the Russians can invade. The workers're too greedy to see . . . .

MARY: All right, don't get excited.

JOE: Where do they think money comes from? Trees? As soon as the wages go up, the prices go up an' you're worse off than when you started. That's right, isn't it?

MARY: I s'pose.

JOE: Course it bloody is. What do they do it for then? Can you tell me that?

MARY: I don't know. Everyone's just tryin' to keep their head above water, I s'pose.

JOE: They don't. Want to destroy the country, that's why. Bloody Communists in the unions. Menzies had the right idea. Ban the lot of 'em. Put 'em all in concentration camps, that's where they belong. It's got to come to a head sooner or later, don't it?

MARY: I don't know what you're so snappy for.

JOE: I'm sorry pet — it's just like — I've left things too long . . . .

MARY: Well, you better get a hold of yourself. You won't be doin' us much good if you go around the bend.

JOE: I'm not goin' round the bend!

MARY: Well, what is it? All this talk about wars an' killin' people. It's not up for us to decide.

JOE: Can't you see what's happenin'?

MARY: I can see what's happenin' to us. You better just start thinkin' about us for once.

JOE: I am thinkin' about you.

MARY: Well why not clean yourself up instead of ravin' 'bout the Communists. You make me frightened sometimes, the way you go on. Gettin' round the house like an old wino. You're startin' to look like an old man. Why don't you have a shave an' put on some clean clothes. That'd be better than talkin' 'bout takin' us all fishing.

[*Pause.*]

JOE: I only want the best for yous.

MARY: I know you do, love, but you've got to keep a grip on reality. If there's gonna be a war or somethin' then I s'pose there's got to be one. There's nothin' we can do about it but try an' make sure the kids are safe. That's what God'd want us to do, isn't it?

JOE: I don't understand any more.

MARY: Look, Joe, nobody understands, you just do what you can and after that it doesn't matter.

[*Blackout.*]

Scene 8

As in scene 6.

DAN: You know how long I was married? Three years. Three fucking years that showed me all the sordid pettiness I could cover myself with. It was like being made to eat your own shit. I was twenty-eight when it was over. I felt like an old and diseased slug. It becomes a world of its own, where every day is a trap that you fall into and every smile or grimace, every small detail of dress and appearance, the food you eat, the stains on the sheets, the itching stench of conversation over the dinner table is like a hook that barbs your eyes and mouth and prick and hangs them up for minute inspection by the traitors within. Every incident is played out again and again so that the maximum pain can be extracted and savoured. Nothing, nothing remains un-noticed or unrecorded. And what does not occur can be imagined so that it also becomes a whip with which you so lovingly flagellate yourself in the empty place where pain is better than nothing. "Did you have a nice day?" she'd ask, "What are you thinking?". "Do you love me?" "What time is it?" Straining like a rope with an imponderable weight. Today. Today. What did you do? Who did you see? That must have been nice — she could never accuse me of being impolite. You masturbate in the toilet because you can't stand to touch her any more, and when she touches you it's like a lizard crawling up your arm. You want to cut it off, and you do. First the arms and the legs. The prick like a little piggy's tail. The guts you hang up for family celebrations. The eyes and ears and tongue you pickle until finally the smorgasbord is prepared and the guests hungry. You eat. There seems no end to the feast.

[*Pause.*]

MIKEY: Why'd you stay together?

DAN: It was more interesting than watching television, and besides, I had something to complain about, which is always reassuring. Christ, I hate this!

MIKEY: What?

DAN: Oh — the little smart-arse in me lurking around the place for just the right opportunity to show me up for the dick-head I am. I've spent half my life apologizing for being such a dead shit and wanting to apologize for apologizing. That must be one of the almighty fucking failures of Christianity: they never teach you to forgive yourself, just the other morons who tread on your toes. I tread on my own toes more than anybody else, and I can't sleep at nights thinking about it. I'm sorry. [*In a different voice.*] Shut up! [*Original voice*] Don't you tell me to shut up! I'm in control. [*Second voice.*] Ah, who gives a stuff, Danny boy. You're just as big a moron as the rest of the loonies. [*Original voice.*] I'm sorry.

[*Blackout.*]

Scene 9

JOE *and* MARY *are sitting on a worn lounge,* MARY *knitting. Long pause at beginning.*

MARY: Peter fell over today. Gee, he's a clumsy kid. Mum said I should take him to the doctor to see if anything's wrong.

[*Pause.*]

Anything on the news.

JOE: No.

[*Pause.*]

MARY: Did I tell you I saw Shirley? She's just had a little girl. She's got four now — all girls. It'll make it hard when they grow up.

JOE: How do you mean?

MARY: Oh, you know — they'll have to have their own rooms.

JOE: Why?

MARY: Girls need their own room when they grow up. We're lucky we've got three boys. [*Pause.*] She said to say hello. [*Pause.*] You were sweet on her one time, weren't you?

JOE: No. What made you think that?

MARY: Didn't you tell me you went out together a couple of times?

JOE: No.

MARY: I thought you did.
    [*Pause.*]

JOE: I mighta gone out with her once. [*Pause.*] You had other boyfriends too but, didn't you?

MARY: Course I did.

JOE: Nothin' wrong with goin' out, is there?

MARY: I didn't say there was. [*Pause.*] Why don't we go to bed, love. Have an early night. [*She puts her hand on his arm. He pulls away.*] What's wrong?

JOE: I might sit up for a while.
    [*Pause.*]

MARY: Do you want me to sit with you?
    [*Pause. She gets up to leave. Cold silence. She exits.*]

JOE: I'll be in in a minute.
    [*Blackout.*]

END OF ACT I

ACT II

Scene 1

Plasto's wine bar the following day (Tuesday 28 April 1959). It is basically a working man's den: one bar, laminex tables, cheap wines and spirits, smoke, filth. Derelicts and semi-criminal types. If possible, a juke box, alternatively a radio, is playing country and western music: Slim Dusty, etc., the tenor of the music being the unfaithfulness of women (e.g., Slim Dusty: "China Doll"). Sordid atmosphere, a lot of which can probably be done with lighting and background noise (e.g., green/yellow lights with high and low spots for interior, a glaring, pale light filtering through the door: sounds of the nearby railway yard, coughing, mumbling, swearing, etc.).
JIMMY, PAT, *and* BEN *are seated on stools by the bar. All are drunk. It is ten in the morning.*
PAT: G'won.
JIMMY: 'S fuckin' true, I tell you. Three fuckin' fingers.
   [*He demonstrates, three fingers being raised and lowered in an obscene manner.*]
PAT: Shoulda told me, you cunt. I wouldn't've minded a piece meself.
JIMMY: Shouldna gone home so early. Told you I was linin' her up.
PAT: You couldn't even walk straight, you fuckin' liar.
JIMMY: Ask fuckin' Ben, he'll tell you. Hey, Ben! Wake up! Wake up, you cunt! Ben!
   [BEN *rouses.*]
BEN: What do you fuckin' want?
JIMMY: Didn't I stick it into that moll last night?
BEN: What fuckin' moll?
PAT: You're fuckin' havin' the DTs again, Jimmy boy. Prob'ly pulled 'imself off in the loo, what do you reckon, Ben?
BEN: Where's my fuckin' drink?
JIMMY: Why don't you go an' fuck yourself! [*He stands up threateningly.*] I done it to her, I tell yous. Rooted the fuckin' arse off her . . . .
   [*He moves off to a table.* JOE *enters. He is wearing his overcoat. He appears uncertain.*]
   . . . You're fuckin' jealous, that's all.

PAT: How much she charge, mate?

JIMMY: Ah, get fucked!

[PAT *sees* JOE.]

PAT: Ay! Joey boy! Over here!

[JOE *comes across.*]

Geez ay! Good to see you, Joey . . .

JOE: G'day Pat.

PAT: Geez haven't seen you for a long time. Ay, I want you to meet me mates — this is me brother — this one here — wake up, you cunt — this one's Ben — Benny the Bender we call him — wake up, you cunt. This is me brother.

BEN: Ay?

PAT: 'S me fuckin' brother.

BEN: Aw, g'day mate.

JOE: G'day.

PAT: Where'd the other cunt go? Aw, fuck him — Geez ay, haven't seen you for a while. Pull up a chair. Hey Lou, gimme brother a drink, will you?

LOU: Who's payin'?

PAT: Who do you think's fuckin' payin'? I am!

JOE: No. Look Pat, I'd better be goin' . . . .

PAT: Fuckin' bullshit. Give 'im a sherry. Grab that chair over there an' come an' talk to your brother. Can't just piss off like that. [*To* LOU] He's me brother, you know. Married, just like I was. You still are, aren't you, Joe?

JOE: Yeah.

PAT: Come on, sit down.

JOE: Oh, all right — I might just stay for one — for old times' sake.

PAT: By geez yeah. Old times, ay? What're you doin' with yourself, Joey?

[LOU *awaits payment for the sherry.*]

JOE: Oh — I lost me job, you know.

PAT: Heard somethin' like that. Jobs a bit hard to come by, ay?

LOU: Well, who's payin'?

PAT: Ay?

LOU: You gonna pay for this or what?

PAT: All right. All right.

[*He fumbles in his trouser pockets and lays a handful of change on the bar.* LOU *counts it out, leaving some.*]

Musta got out o' the wrong side of the bed this mornin'. No work, you say.

JOE: No.

PAT: 'S a bastard, ain't it? All fuckin' Holt's fault. Prick doesn't know what he's doin'. Must be gettin' a bit tight, ay? How's Mary?

JOE: Yeah, she's good.

PAT: Geez, she was a nice girl, Joey. Hold on to that one. Fuckin' beauty.

[*Pause.*]

JOE: How's yourself?

PAT: Me? I'm all right. Some bludger hit me over the head an' stole me money last Friday. I know who it was, but. I'll get the cunt. You don't look too happy, matey.

JOE: I'm just a bit worried, you know.

PAT: How much they givin' you?

JOE: Five quid.

PAT: Five quid — an' there's fuckin' Menzies give himself twelve quid extra just for sittin' on his arse. Give you the shits, wouldn't it? You like a loan or somethin'.

JOE: No — No, I'm OK. Got to get somethin' sooner or later.

PAT: Sure you will. It's a fuckin' mugs' game, ain't it, Joey? Workin'. Jesus Christ, might as well be a fuckin' animal as spend your life in a factory. [*Pause.*] One day them cunts'll get theirs, I tell you. There'll be a fuckin' revolution or some fuckin' thing an' they'll be hangin' just like they hung old Ned. Cunts. [*Pause.*] Yeah, drink up. Plenty o' time for that. An' Mary's good, you say?

JOE: Yeah, she's all right.

PAT: Geez, you got a prize there, Joey.

JOE: Yeah, I s'pose.

PAT: Too fuckin' right you did. Geez, if I had someone like her there'd be no lookin' back.

[*Pause.*]

JOE: Yeah, I dunno . . . .

PAT: What?

JOE: Oh. [*Pause.*] I'm just feelin' — you know — a bit tied down, I s'pose.

[*Pause.*]

PAT: Ah, it's nothin' to be worried about. Everybody feels that way once in a while. Don't matter whether you're married or not.

[*Pause.*]

JOE: Yeah.

[*Pause.*]

PAT: Sure they do. If you're not married you got a job, if you ain't got a job you're up the shit or in jail. It's all the same. Don't matter what it is — you're always tied down to somethin'.
[*Pause.*]

JOE: Yeah, I know .... It's just ... You can't do nothin'.... You can't do what you want, you know. Always have to be thinkin' 'bout the kids or somethin'.

PAT: Depends on what you want to do, I s'pose.
[*Pause.*]

JOE: What's it like, Pat?

PAT: What?

JOE: Oh, you know. With other women.

PAT: When you're married, you mean?

JOE: Yeah.

PAT: Not worth the trouble, matey. Not worth the flamin' trouble.
[*One of the men sitting at a table with a woman and another man breaks a glass and holds it threateningly at the man. All conversation stops, background noise as before: music, railway, etc. Pause.*]

FIRST MAN: I just told you, all right.

SECOND MAN [*placatingly*]: Yeah, all right. Don't get upset.

FIRST MAN: I'm not gettin' upset. I'm just tellin' you what's what.

SECOND MAN: All right.
[*Pause.*]

FIRST MAN: All right. An' don't let me catch you again. An' you get it straight, all right? Because I'd fuckin' put this through you now if I thought you was gonna do it again. All right?

SECOND MAN: All right, all right.
[*Pause.* FIRST MAN *lowers the glass and stirs a slop with his finger. Their conversation continues in a low, tense manner.*]

FIRST MAN: All right.
[*Pause.*]

PAT: Yeah. [*Pause.*] You want another?

JOE: Ay?

PAT: Another drink?

JOE: Another drink? Oh, yeah. Yeah.

PAT: Two more, Lou.

LOU: Two more?

PAT: Yeah.

[*Pause.* LOU *serves the drinks and takes the money from the bar.*]

PAT: What was we talkin' about?

JOE: Oh. . . . It doesn't matter.

PAT: Oh, that's right. Yeah, fuckin' around. Bad for the appetite, take my word.
[*Pause.*]

JOE: It's just . . . I feel funny, you know. I don't know how to explain it. . . . You wouldn't tell Mary I said this, would you?

PAT: Listen matey, it ain't even worth talkin' about. You ain't no different to nobody else — Mary prob'ly thinks the same things sometimes.

JOE: Oh, no . . . . No, she wouldn't.

PAT: Why the fuck not? She's human ain't she?

JOE: No, she wouldn't.

PAT: Everybody does. It's natural. Don't do no harm to think about. Geez.
[*Pause.*]

JOE: You think?

PAT: As long as that's all it is. I tell you somethin' but, Joey: You don't know what hell is till you start doin' it. Jesus, you can't enjoy a fuckin' thing . . . .
[FIRST MAN *stands suddenly and leaves.*]
. . . Always lookin' over your shoulder to see who's behind you. Fuck me. You'd be a bloody mug if you ever started that sort of caper.
[*Pause.*]

JOE: I just don't get no satisfaction no more, you know. Don't even feel like doin' it half the time.

PAT: Playin' round's not gonna help, I tell you. [*Pause.*] Look, I got this book, an' it shows you different ways of doin' it, like. I'll give you a lend if you want.

JOE [*alarmed*]: No, Mary wouldn't do things like that.

PAT: How do you know if you haven't even talked to her? Jesus, if you're feelin' like that, how do you think she feels?

JOE: No, no I couldn't ask her to do stuff like that.

PAT: What? You'd root some moll down a ditch somewhere to save yourself a red face with your wife? Jesus, that's a funny way of lookin' at things.
[*Pause.*]

JOE: I dunno, Pat. I feel real confused. It's like — it's like bein'
dead sometimes. I dunno what to do.
[*Pause.*]

PAT: Yeah, well, I dunno what to tell you. [*Pause.*] Just be
careful you don't end up with nothin'.
[*Blackout.*]

*The following seven scenes are cameo shots of the bar as the
day progresses into evening. The setting remains essentially
the same: people come and go, move around, perhaps the
lighting becomes increasingly intense and glaring.*

Scene 2

A short time later. JOE *has perhaps bought some fish and chips.*

PAT [*laughing*]: You shoulda seen im. Want to fight me, mate?
This little skeleton of a bloke — a puff o' wind' d blow 'im
down, pissed as a parrot. Want to fight me, mate?
[*Blackout.*]

Scene 3

As before. BENNY *missing.*

JOE: Oh, he was a good fighter, Pat. Never seen anyone like him.
Geez, big broad shoulders. Strong legs. When he walked,
people'd stop an' stare. An' geez, couldn't he lay 'em out.
[*Blackout.*]

Scene 4

Room empty except for PAT, JOE, *and* LOU.

PAT: I can still remember the fuckin' judge lookin' down his snoot
at me like as if I was a shit someone done on the floor.
Fuckin' first offence an' they locked me up. Opens your eyes
to what's goin' on, I tell you.

JOE: Why didn't you go straight, Pat?

PAT: Go fuckin' straight. Who's straight? You tell me one bloke
that don't cheat on his tax or knock off stuff from work. Go

straight. I got caught. That's the only difference between me an' you, Joey. Don't start preachin' to me.
[*Blackout.*]

Scene 5

JIMMY *sitting with them again.*
JOE: You got to be strong, that what it is. You got to be a man. That's the only way you ever get anything in this world.
[*Blackout.*]

Scene 6

JIMMY *and* BEN *sitting together at another table.* JOE *and* PAT *at the bar.*
PAT: If there's a fuckin' god, why don't he do somethin' about them fuckin' starvin' kids you're always readin' about. He'd be a fuckin' mean cunt, wouldn't he? Fuckin' God.
[*Pause.*]
JOE: I dunno. . . . I just reckon there's got to be some . . . intelligence . . . somethin' behind it all.
PAT: I'll fuckin' tell you who's behind it. It's the fuckin' chairman of BHP and all his mates. They're the cunts behind it.
[*Pause.*] They're the cunts.
[*Blackout.*]

Scene 7

JOE *and* PAT *sitting at a table.* JOE *crying.*
JOE: You know I'd never do anything to hurt you, you know that, don't you?
PAT: It's all right, matey.
JOE: You're me brother, ain't you — me own flesh an' blood. I wouldn't ever do nothin' like that to you.
PAT: We got to stick together, all the Brimmy brothers.
JOE: I love you, Pat.
[*Blackout.*]

Scene 8

JIMMY, BEN, PAT *and* JOE *sitting together at a table.*

PAT: Somethin' wrong with 'is fuckin' mind. Not a word an' there's this fuckin' eighteen-inch carvin' knife. Prob'ly had a blue with 'is missus or somethin'. Cunt.
[*The song "High Noon" begins to play.*]

JOE: Oh, listen to this, boys. Beautiful song.
[JOE *leans back, listening. "High Noon" becomes the dominant sound. Lights dim slowly. While the song is playing, everyone but* JOE *and* PAT *leave. Edit the song down to the appropriate length. It finishes.*]

JOE: Geez that's a good song.

PAT: Come on, Joe. Got to go home.

JOE: Ay?

PAT: They closed up. Got to go home.

JOE: What time is it?

PAT: Closing time.

JOE: Is it that late already? Oh, geez, Mary'll be worried. Better go home, ay?

PAT: Yeah.

JOE: Why not come back to my place? We can play some of the old records an' have a feed.

PAT: Yeah, why not. Gettin' a bit peckish. Won't Mary mind?

JOE: You're me brother, ain't you?

PAT: Let's go then.
[PAT *picks up a flagon of red which is on the table.*]

JOE: Yeah. . . . Where'd I put the keys? Oh, here they are. Right. Let's go then, ay? [*Sings*] Do not forsake me, oh my darlin' . . .
[*Blackout.*]

Scene 9

The kitchen. Lights up on MARY *in dressing-gown, sitting. Her appearance is a combination of fear and worry.* JOE'S *arrival is heralded by the sound of stumbling and swearing outside: "Where's the fuckin' key?", "Hold on, matey, I'll just take a leak", etc. Open scene with pause.*
The sound effects from this scene on will become increasingly

*complex. For this particular scene, it has two streams: (1)
Background music, as is perhaps coming from an adjacent
house: e.g., Johnny O'Keefe ("Shout", "Rock around the clock",
etc.) or Elvis Presley. This should be played sufficiently loud as
to be distracting; (2) a cello and wind bell struck randomly, but
also sparely.*

MARY: Who's there?

JOE: Mary? It's me, Joe.

> [*She quickly unlocks the door and embraces him.*]

MARY: Oh Joe, where have you been?

> [PAT *enters, carrying the flagon.*]

JOE: I brung me brother home. You know Pat, don't you?

PAT: G'day Mary.

> [*Pause.*]

MARY: Hello, Pat.

JOE: Go on, give him a kiss. All the same family now.

MARY [*To* JOE]: You've been down the pub.

JOE: Yeah, we had a few drinks. Go on, give him a kiss.

PAT: Oh, no Joe . . . .

MARY: You been down the pub all this time.

PAT: Oh, look Mary, it was my . . . .

JOE [*angrily*]: Kiss me brother!

> [MARY *slaps Joe's face. Pause. She turns her back.*]

MARY: Why didn't you tell me! Why didn't you! Why! [*Crying*] I
thought you might've been killed. Why did you do it to me!

JOE: Do I have to ask your permission to go out now?

MARY: You could at least show me the courtesy of telling me
whether or not you'll be home for tea.

> [*Pause.*]

JOE: I — I didn't realize it was so late. I'm sorry. [*Pause.*] It was
an accident. Honest to God, Mary, I didn't mean to upset
you. Thought you'd be in bed by now. I shoulda thought. It
just sort o' slipped away.

> [*Pause.*]

MARY [*crying*]: I didn't know what to think, Joe. I was so
frightened . . . .

> [*He puts his arm around her.*]

JOE: It's all right, pet. Don't cry, everything's all right.

> [*She composes herself and pulls away.*]

MARY: How did you get home?

JOE: Drove.

MARY: Wonder you didn't kill someone. Look at you; can't even stand straight.

JOE: Couldn't leave it there. Mighta got stolen.

MARY: Better it be stolen than kill some innocent.

JOE: I was real careful, wasn't I, Pat?

PAT: Oh, yeah. Yeah.

JOE: . . . Come home on the back roads. We was extra careful.

MARY: I rung up the police an' the hospitals. How was I supposed to know what you were doin'?
  [*Pause.*]

JOE: Well, we're both here in one piece, ain't we?

MARY: You stink of wine. How long were you down there?

JOE: Only a few hours.

MARY: You been lookin' for work all this time, have you?

JOE: All right. I got there before lunch.

MARY: All day in the pub. It's come to a fine pass, hasn't it. S'pose you spent all the money.

JOE: Anybody'd think I go down the pub every day.

MARY: You had no right to make me worry! You've got no right!
  [*Pause.*] At least the kids're asleep. I'd hate for them to see you like this.

JOE: Jesus Christ, Mary. Can't a man have a good time for once.

MARY: It's all right for you. Go an' spend all the money at the pub while I have to stay here with the kids. When was the last time I had a good time?

JOE: Can't you leave me alone!

MARY: What would've happened if you'd've been killed? What would I have done with three kids to look after. You never think of anyone but yourself.

JOE: Shut up! Just shut up, will you! [*Pause.*] Look, I was just feelin' a bit bad, that's all. [*Pause.*] Didn't have no accident. What's there to argue about? I said I was sorry, didn't I?
  [*Pause.*]

MARY: You eaten yet?
  [*Pause.*]

JOE: No.
  [*Pause.*]

MARY: S'pose you want a meal, do you?

PAT: Oh, look, I might go home . . . .

MARY: Suit yourself.

JOE: Oh, come on Pat. Have somethin' to eat first.
[*Pause.*]
MARY: You're here now. Might as well have somethin'. You can
have Joe's tea between yous. Sausages an' chips. That all
right with you?
JOE: Come on.
PAT: Yeah, all right. That'd be real good, Mary.
JOE: Good boy, good boy. . . . Oh, she's a wonderful little girl, ain't
she, Pat?
PAT: She's a treasure, Joe, a real treasure.
[*They stand awkwardly. An uncomfortable silence.*]
JOE: Ah, let's sit down, ay Pat?
PAT: Yeah, yeah. Good idea.
[*Pause.*]
JOE: I was thinkin' I'd play some records for Pat, ay Mary? Some
of the old songs.
MARY: You'll wake the kids.
[*Pause.*]
JOE: We'll have it on real low, sweety. Kids won't hear.
MARY: They will.
JOE: We'll close the door.
MARY: You know what a light sleeper Mikey is. It's a wonder he
hasn't woken up already.
JOE: Oh, just one — a soft one — "Begin the Beguine". You like
that one.
MARY: I said no.
[*Pause.* PAT *appears ready to bolt.*]
PAT: Look, I might go home — feelin' pretty tired . . . .
JOE: No, sit down Pat.
[*Pause.* PAT *resumes his seat.*]
PAT: Where's the toilet, Joe?
JOE: Just through the door, on your left.
MARY: Don't pull the chain. You'll wake the kids.
PAT: Anything you say, Mary. First on the left, ay?
JOE: That's right Pat.
[PAT *exits. Pause.*]
MARY [*in a whisper*]: Why'd you bring him home for?
JOE: I thought you might let us play some of the old records.
MARY: You know I don't like him bein' in the house.
JOE: He's my brother.
MARY: He's got a filthy mouth and I don't want him around the
kids.

JOE: He minds his language when he's here.

MARY: I don't care. I don't want him in the house when I'm here, all right?

JOE: Jesus Christ.

MARY: That's nice language, isn't it. He's a bad influence on you, Joe. I wish you'd keep away from him.

JOE: Oh, come on Mary. Let's make up. I don't like fightin' with you all the time.
[*Sound of toilet flushing. Pause. Baby begins to wail. Pause.* PAT *enters sheepishly.*]

PAT: I'm real sorry, Mary. I forgot . . . .

MARY: It's all right.
[MARY *exits through the same door.* PAT *sits down.* JOE *shrugs. Pause.*]

PAT: She's a bit crook, ain't she.

JOE: It's my fault. Shoulda come home earlier.

PAT: Don't know how many times I said that. Mighta still been married if I'd taken any notice, too.
[*Pause.*]

JOE: What was your wife's name again, Pat?

PAT: Stella.
[*Pause.*]

JOE: You ever see her now?

PAT: No. [*Pause.*] Last I heard she was off with some bloke in Queensland.

JOE: She take the kids, did she?

PAT: Yeah. Took the lot.
[*Pause.*]

JOE: They're not like sausages cooked out in the open, are they, Pat? Everything tastes different in the bush. Fresh or something.

PAT: Yeah. No denying that.

JOE: Sausages an' chips an' then a billy full of tea an' some damper. That's what Dad used to have, weren't it — sometimes he'd tell me. Campin' under the trees. No one for miles. Just you an' the bush. When he got cold, he'd get some rocks an' heat 'em up in the fire an' then he'd dig a hole an' put 'em in an' cover it up, an' that'd be his bed. Catch fish sometimes — big rainbow trout. Beautiful. And the wild fruits whenever you want. Blackberries an' quince, anything you want. [*Pause.*] Why'd you come back for, Pat?

PAT: Ay?

JOE: Why'd you come back to the city for?

PAT: Oh, I dunno. Was different when Harry died. Bloke needs some company, s'pose. [*Pause.*] Snags. That's what we used to call 'em. Snags. Have 'em for breakfast sometimes. Bit of tomato sauce. Slice o' bread an' butter. Bloody beauty. Get 'em for meself whenever I think about it.... I let meself run down, that's the trouble. Got to be fit to hack it out there. It'd kill me now.

JOE: Oh, you're still as strong as you ever was.

PAT: Yeah? How much you reckon I'd weigh?

JOE: I dunno.... Twelve stone ....

PAT: Give it a break. Down to nine an' a half.

JOE: Oh, you're only kiddin' me ....

PAT: Look at me bloody arm. [*Pulls up his coat and shirt sleeve.*] Bloody flesh just fallen off these last couple o' years. Don't eat right, that's why. [*Pause.*] Thought I was bloody king shit — sorry — thought I was gonna be a big man, you know. Yeah. Well, I done all right for meself — got me own house, you know — so I can't complain. Better off than some blokes, that's for sure.
[*Pause.*]

JOE: You're your own man now, ain't you.

PAT: You'd be a hard cuss to please, wouldn't you. Bloody beautiful wife an' three kids an' you're still not happy. Lot o' blokes be glad to change places with you. I met a few of 'em too. [*Lowers his voice.*] Get a fuck whenever you want, have your washin' done for you. All your meals cooked. Jesus, what more could you want?
[*Pause.*]

JOE: Yeah, but you ain't free.

PAT: Bloody free. Jesus. You show me one cunt that's free. Fuckin' dead men, they're the only ones. Harry's free, an' you an' me'll be with him soon enough.
[*Pause. The baby is by now quiet.*]

JOE: It's just ... I don't feel like a man no more.... I just want to get out sometimes. Go to the bush —
[*During the following, fade out background noise, while at the same time bring in a number of violins playing a sustained, high pitched note, which carries over into the following scene.*]

PAT [*interrupting*]: Bloody bush. I'll tell you what the bloody bush is. Bloody blowflies in your meat an' ants in your sugar, that's what the bloody bush is. You live like a bloody king here. Fuckin' fridge an' stove. No worries 'bout the food goin' off or gettin' wood to cook it with. No bringin' water up the bloody hill from the creek. Got everything you want. Go to the races whenever you like. Pub just down the street. Go to the pictures. Fuckin' doctor handy. Shops, electricity. Whatever you bloody want. You reckon the old man liked it trampin' round the country lookin' for work? Nothin' but a hobo, that's what he was. Out in the wet an' the cold. Away from home without a fuckin' razoo to his name. That the sort of life you want?

[*Blackout.*]

Scene 10

As in act I, scene 6. The two "guards" are still present. Fade the violin sound through the first few lines. While at the same time introducing the sound of bees swarming. This terminates with the clock striking the quarter hour in an adjacent room — this is a normal clock chime which in some way is slightly distorted, e.g., the intervals between the chimes are not uniform. General background noise as before: light rain, the occasional car, an intermittent siren in the distance.

DAN: Yeah, I'm just feeling a bit whacko at the moment. A profound sense of boredom. The strange and terrible legacy that has been passed from father to son along with the other miseries of influenza, cancer, coronary occlusions, and events of world importance. Our father must have been the most bored man on earth. Have you ever thought of that?

MIKEY: No.

DAN: No — I mean it. Too frightened to talk and too arrogant to listen. Try to engage him in political dialogue about something unimportant like the war in Vietnam, and he'd snarl from behind his "I vote Liberal" all purpose, weatherproof motto with which he could even refuse to pass the salt if so desired. Can you imagine anything more ridiculous than an unskilled labourer voting Liberal? I s'pose he was glad when they decided to dump the whole thing and disband parliament, was he?

[*Pause.*]

MIKEY: He didn't say anything.

DAN: No, he wouldn't. The great stone wall. Hiding inside an impregnable fortress of cultivated stupidity. A good, honest, God-fearing man who wanted the gooks slaughtered as quickly and efficiently as possible, with the best of modern technology. A paid-up member of the working class with the nous of a dinosaur lumbering into the Ice Age. Well, he got what he wanted, didn't he. Law and fucking order, respect for your superiors and ten thousand under lock and key. I bet you he'd turn me over to the cops if I did go an' see him.

[*Pause.*]

MIKEY: You're not going to?

[*Pause.*]

DAN: Why the fuck should I? To sit staring at him wondering what to say? To wait for some glimmer of recognition. I'm disturbed enough as it is without looking at what I'm going to be like in thirty years time. It's like having a worm in your gut that you know's gonna crawl out of your nose one day while you're looking at your greying hairs in the mirror. I'll change my name to Joe and hand myself over to the nearest loony bin for care and supervision and a daily dose of some strong tranquillizer that might keep the disease in check. The man who was swallowed by his father, a case study in terminal illness.

[*Pause. The clock chimes, as above.*]

What's the old house like now?

MIKEY: Oh, I dunno — the same. Dad doesn't do much work on it. Sometimes he'll spend a couple o' days doin' a bit of paintin' or somethin'. [*Pause.*] Why didn't you come to the funeral?

[*Pause.*]

DAN: I didn't get your message till the following day. [*Pause.*] How did he take it?

MIKEY: He cried a bit.

[*Pause.*]

DAN: Did she say anything?

[*Pause.*]

MIKEY: She wanted to see you.

[*Pause.*]

DAN: You know — when I was a kid, I used to tell them that when I grew up I'd be rich, and I'd buy them a big house where they'd never have to get out o' bed. We'd all live in the big house together. [*Pause. Suddenly*] Yeah, well it's gone now. You still play footy?

MIKEY: Yeah, oh geez, we had a good game last week. Against Cronulla, you know. Nearly got sent off but.

DAN [*bemused*]: What'd you do?

MIKEY: Oh, this bloke hit me in the scrum, you know. Right on the nose. Boy, did it hurt. Yeah, so I stiff-armed 'im. Musta nearly broke his neck, I reckon. [*They both laugh.*] I made out it was an accident but, so he just give me a warnin'. Serves 'em right. That's a real dirty trick, hittin' someone in a scrum. Both me arms were up, you know. Couldn't protect myself. That'll teach him.

DAN: Dirty bastard. You think you'll make it into the finals?

MIKEY: Oh, I dunno. Maybe. Depends on what happens next week. The coach reckons we will, but I dunno. There's some good teams. You play any more?

DAN [*laughs*]: Me? No, haven't played for years.... Hey — what was the name of that mate of yours? The little woppo that was peddlin' dope to the Boy Scouts?

MIKEY: Calogero?

DAN: Calogero, that's right. Whatever happened to him?

MIKEY: He joined the army, last I heard.

DAN: Yeah, shit eh. What'd he do that for?

MIKEY: I dunno — didn't have a job, I think.

DAN: Geez. [*Turning to the "guards"*] You hear that? That's what you fellas should do instead of wastin' your health in a rat-trap like this.

[*Sound of bottles breaking. Drunken woman:* "Oh, ya silly old maggot"; *drunken man:* "shudup!"]

Yeah, give it to the old slut, you sonofabitch. Whacko the diddle-oh. [*Sings*] ... And he kicked her once again. Oh, a drunken man is a happy man, a drunken man is free. Crazy morons. [*Parodying the demonstration chant.*] What do we want? [*In a different voice*] More piss! [*Original voice, alternating with second voice*] When do we want it! Now! The people — united — will never be defeated! The people — united — will never be defeated! — Hooray fuck. [*Takes a gulp of the vodka.*] The people! [*To the guards*] What're you creeps hanging round for anyway? Aren't you missing out on Mickey Mouse or something?

[*They stand and leave without acknowledging him.*]

Don't strain yourselves trying to follow the plot.

[*They close the door after them.*]

That's what Karl Marx does to a potential human being.
[*Yelling out after them*] You pinko bastards! You tell 'em
a joke an' they've got to work out whether or not it's right
line before they'll laugh. [*Sings to the tune of "The Red
Flag"*] The working class can kiss my arse, I've got the
foreman's job at last. .... Ah, they gimme the shits.

[*Pause.*]

Well, that was exciting, wasn't it.

MIKEY: Who're they?

DAN: Two characters in search of an author for all I know. Ex-
catholics for sure — they find out that God's dead and join
the Resistance to expiate their guilt. No, I don't know.
Heavy little cunts but, aren't they? Prob'ly think I'm a spy.
Yeah, God, what a way to spend a life — surrounded by
lunatics and paranoiacs. Thank the Lord for the plumbers
and labourers of the world. Put a bit of sanity into the
place. [*Sings*] Nobody knows the trouble I've seen. Nobody
knows but Jesus.

[*Pause.*]

MIKEY: You in any sort of trouble.?

DAN: Trouble? I'm up to my fucking eyeballs in trouble! The cops
want to cut me up into little bits, the comrades want to
hand me over to the cops, an' my mother's dead. That
enough trouble for you? [*Pause.*] Look, about three
months ago we got offered a few seats in parliament...

MIKEY: Parliament? They gonna have an election?

DAN: Wait for it. We got offered a few lousy seats in some
mythical parliament if we called off the sabotage campaign
and guaranteed that there'd be no strikes after we were
legalized — as if we could dictate to the workers. See, the
theory goes that the only rationale the military's got for
maintaining the dictatorship is that the Communists'll
plunge the country into civil war as soon as the iron grip is
loosened. Which is bullshit — and they know it's bullshit.
The only effective thing the Left's done in the last eighteen
months is rip the shit out of one another in the interests of
doctrinal purity or some fucking thing. So anyway, the old
parliamentary parties want to make a deal: we agree to
their rules and they'll give a few officials a steady income
for the rest of their lives.

MIKEY: I don't understand. Don't you want an election?

DAN: Why? There's no going back now. You think there'll ever be another socialist government while the military's watching from the wings. The fight's in the open now — any return to parliamentary democracy will be a defeat for the working class, and they'd never forgive us. And the damn thing is that we could win, if we could only stick together, we could fucking win. [*Pause.*] You'd think they'd fucking learn, wouldn't you. A full-blown fascist dictatorship and the little cretins are still fighting among themselves. The Trots want to murder the Stalinists, the Stalinists want to murder each other, and everyone wants to murder the Maoists. Not to mention the anarchists, the Castroites, the socialists, the feminists and the Gay Liberation Front. Jesus Christ. The people united.

[*Pause.*]

MIKEY: Why not get out?

DAN [*savagely*]: How can I fucking get out!

[*Blackout.*]

Scene 11

As in act I, scene 9. MARY *sitting alone. Musical background noise as in act II, scene 9, but more subdued. In addition, there is a low, colourless, staccato type "conversation" being carried out — e.g., the exchanges over a taxi radio. Perhaps infrequently, the drone of flies. Other noises as indicated in the text.*

[*Pause.* JOE *enters.*]

JOE: Mary?

[*Pause. He comes closer.*]

JOE: What's the matter?

MARY: Nothing.

[*Pause. He sits beside her.*]

JOE: Why don't you come out an' sit with us.

MARY: I just want to be alone for a while.

[*Pause.*]

JOE: You still cranky with me? [*Pause.*] I told you I was sorry, didn't I? [*Pause.*] I just' didn't think, that's all. It won't happen again, I promise you, sweety. [*Pause.*] Oh, come on.

[*Pause.*]

MARY: Why did you ask me to kiss Pat?
  [*Pause.*]
JOE: I dun — I dunno — I wasn't thinkin'.
MARY: Were you tryin' to make fun of me?
JOE: No, no — I wouldn't do that. You know I wouldn't do that, don't you?
  [*Pause.*]
MARY: Well, why'd you do it for?
  [*Pause.*]
JOE: I dunno.
  [*Pause.*]
MARY: You're still happy with me, aren't you Joe?
JOE: Course I am. Course I am, sweety.
  [*Pause.*]
MARY: You never show it any more. [*Pause.*] Why wouldn't you come to bed with me the other night?
JOE: I was just feelin' a bit depressed. I love you, Mary — you should know that.
  [*Pause.*]
MARY: You haven't touched me for months.
  [*Pause.*]
JOE: I just haven't been feelin' too good, that's all.
MARY: It was never the same after the kids came along.
JOE: They were your idea.
MARY: You fathered them. I didn't do that by meself.
  [*Pause.*]
JOE: I told you, didn't I. You didn't care. All you wanted to do was get married an' have a baby.
MARY: What's wrong with that? I never wanted anything else, even when I was a kid.
JOE: Bringin' children into a world like this.
MARY: We loved them.
JOE: If we loved 'em we would've smothered 'em at birth.
MARY: How can you say that?
JOE: Look at the place. Wars an' starvation. Is that the sort of future you wanted for 'em? Is that what they'll thank us for. Better off dead.
MARY: It's always been like that. There's always been wars. That's what life is.
JOE: God help us.
  [*Pause.*]

MARY: The other day, I had to get something out of the garage —
a screwdriver — I was gonna fix up the cupboard — I found
a magazine, with pictures of girls in it. Was it yours?

JOE: No. What would I do with somethin' like that? It musta got
mixed up with somethin' else. Why would I want somethin'
like that!
[*Pause.*]

MARY: I know you bought it, Joe.

JOE: Oh, no Mary — I swear to you, it wasn't mine. Maybe I
picked it up by mistake somewhere. No, geez, you got to
believe me.
[*Pause.*]

MARY: I know men get these thoughts sometimes. It just hurt me a
bit to find it like that.

JOE: Oh, Mary, I'd rather be struck dead than lie to you about
something like that. I promise you truly, it wasn't mine.
[*Pause.*]

MARY: What's happening to us, Joe? [*Pause.*] Are you sorry we
got married?

JOE: Why are you asking me all these questions? I feel like I'm on
trial or somethin'. I'm still with you, aren't I?

MARY: It's just like two strangers livin' in the same house. We
hardly ever talk — you won't come near me. [*Pause.*] Have
you got someone else?

JOE: No, I haven't got anyone else.

MARY: Well what is it then? Don't you think I need you any more?

JOE: I been worried — everything's pilin' up. I dunno, it's just —
like everything's goin' against us.

MARY: I know it is, love, but it's got to get better sooner or later,
hasn't it?

MARY: Why not come to bed?

JOE: No — no, I'll wait up a little while with Pat.

MARY: All right. I'll wait up too.

JOE: Why?

MARY: Why not? I might as well be out with you two as in bed
alone.
[*Pause.*]

JOE: I know I been no good for you.

MARY: I love you, Joe, that's good enough.
[*Pause.*]

JOE: I wouldn't blame you if you left me.
[*Pause.*]

MARY: Is that what you want?

JOE: No — no, I need you. God knows how much I need you. It just seems like an awful life for you. Havin' to put up with me.

[*Pause.*]

MARY: Are you sorry we got married? [*Pause. She turns slightly away.*] We could always get a divorce.

JOE: I don't want you to leave me, Mary.

MARY: I don't think you know what you want.

JOE: Oh, help me please, can't you.

MARY: Well, what am I supposed to do? Hang around here like an old maid till you make up your mind whether you want me or not?

JOE: I do want you.

[*Pause.*]

MARY: Well, I don't know what to do.

[*Pause.*]

JOE: You could get someone else.

[*Pause.*]

MARY: What?

JOE: I'm no good for you, Mary. I only make you unhappy.

MARY: I don't understand. Are you saying that you want me to live with you, but sleep with someone else? Is that what you're saying? [*Pause.*] You could live like that? [*Pause.*] Well I tell you now, I couldn't.

JOE: Well what can we do? I'm impotent!

MARY: Oh, don't be stupid. How could you be?

[*Pause. The sound of bees swarming, increasing in volume.*]

JOE: I can't get excited any more.

MARY: Have you been to the doctor?

JOE: No.

MARY: Well, how do you know till you've been to the doctor?

JOE: I know the way I feel.

[*Pause.*]

MARY: Don't you find me attractive any more? [*Pause.*] Oh, Joe, how did we come to this? Is it my fault?

JOE: No — it's nobody's fault.

MARY: You're lying. You're only saying this because you want someone else yourself.

JOE: No, Mary — I'd never do anything like that to you.

MARY: No, but you want me to so you won't feel guilty. That's it, isn't it. All this talk about bein' no good for me an' how you wouldn't blame me if I left you. You haven't got the courage to make a decision yourself, have you? Oh, you're such a selfless person, Joe, such a generous man — all right, if that's the way you want it . . . . [*She stands up.*]

[*Lights begin to illuminate* DAN, *who is sitting moodily aware of the scene. He remains, however, shadowy.*]

JOE: No, Mary — you've got it all wrong. That's not what I meant at all.

MARY: Are you gonna come out, or are you gonna sit here feelin' sorry for yourself. I've had enough cryin' an' worryin'. It's about time I started thinkin' about meself.

[*Blackout everything except* DAN.]

[*A pastiche of sounds which should warp into and through one another. There should be various levels, for example:* DAN'S *speech, indicated below, could be a substratum of sound which comes into focus and then dips beneath other noises, such as the chants, the sound of pigeons, etc. The following is only a suggestion: the loud slamming of a engine being coupled to a carriage, together with the sound of workmen's voices shouting commands, steam, etc.* DAN'S *voice over a megaphone, reverberating in what appears to be a large space, and heard from a distance.* "What happened in Italy in the twenties . . . and Germany in the thirties . . ." *Sound of men marching, with someone barking orders.* ". . . is happening here today." *Voices in a demonstration chant:* "The people — united — will never be defeated. The people — united —" *Sound of soldiers running.* FIRST MAN: "Hasn't got very big tits, has she?" SECOND MAN: "Give us a feel your cunt." DAN: "The arrests, the torture and murders . . ." *A few phrases from a Brandenburg Concerto* ". . . must be met with . . ." *Sporadic rifle fire. A sustained note from a violin. A number of men barking crisply together:* "Hile hile hile hile . . ." *(the word they shout is irrelevant, as long as it is short, meaningless, rapid, and sinister.) A woman singing weakly:* "As we go marching, marching . . ." *(The song the woman sings is "Bread and Roses", the words and music of which can be found in most feminist songbooks.)* DAN: ". . . armed resistance which will be satisfied with nothing less . . ." *Rapid gunfire. The voice of an aged African or Indian man:* ". . . till you experience your first massacres, and you will."

Woman's voice, as above: "... in the beauty of the day, a million darkened kitchens, a thousand mill lofts grey..."
DAN: "... than the revolutionary overthrow of capitalism."
FIRST MAN: "Where is he?" *Woman singing:* "... are touched with all the radiance that a sudden sun discloses." *Woman screams.*]
[*Cut all sound.*]
[*Blackout.*]

Scene 12

As in scene 10. MIKEY *is apparently asleep.* DAN *is more agitated, periodically wiping the right side of his forehead with his open palm.*

DAN: I used to be frightened — of getting arrested, you know. There's no time any more. It sort of curls up and dies inside you. After a while you can't feel yourself. You do something and five minutes later you can't remember what. It's like being lowered into eternity where everything happens at once but nothing changes. Time embraces you and then one night leaves you in some sordid hotel room wondering what your name is and how come you didn't drive a truck. Your hands shake — you can't light a match or something like that. You don't eat because you haven't got the time, and then you begin to forget to eat. You sleep in your clothes, you begin to smell, your skin turns grey. You watch it all with a mild sense of curiosity and distaste. Healthy, vibrant people enjoying themselves look like monsters. You can't stand to talk to people. And slowly the things that caused you to join the struggle — the compassion, the outrage at injustice — die, and you become a much more ugly and diseased thing. That's what happened to Gris. The cops didn't kill him. They can hang up his body till it turns green, he'd already crawled out of it and climbed into the chants and the songs and the posters. Did you see 'em? The day they got him the streets were plastered: "We are with you Ramon Gris!" — I saw him a week ago — A revolutionary's got nothing. No family, no friends, no children or lovers. You kill them inside you so they can't be hurt or hurt the revolution. The revolution, comrade. Not the Vietnamese revolution, not the Irian Jaya revolution,

but The Revolution. It sure is funny comin' back to nothin',
ain't it, Danny boy? You fuckin' said it, buddy. Sure is
fuckin' funny. Haw fuckin' haw.
[*Blackout.*]

Scene 13

The kitchen. The flagon is still on the table. Pause after lights up.
MARY *enters briskly, with a forced cheerfulness.*

MARY: What's everyone looking so sad about? Anybody'd think
 someone'd died. How about opening the wine, Pat? We'll
 have a party.

PAT: Ay?

MARY: A party. What can we celebrate? Nine years of wedded
 bliss, how's that?
 [JOE *enters.*]

MARY: Well, if it isn't Sad Sack himself. Sit down, lover boy, you
 look as if you're about to fall apart. A bit slow on opening
 the bottle, aren't you, Pat?

PAT: Ay? Oh, right. Anything you say, Mary.
 [*He opens the bottle. She gets two glasses.*]

MARY: We should have party hats and balloons [*suddenly
 remembering*] and music!
 [*She turns on the radio, which blares out some popular
 love song.*]

JOE: What about Mikey?

MARY: Oh, you can look after him, can't you my little pet?

PAT: You not havin' a drink, Joe?

MARY: No, he's gonna look after the kids, aren't you sweety.

JOE: What're you tryin' to do, Mary?

MARY: I'm just havin' a quiet drink with me brother, sweety pie.
 Why? Anything wrong?

JOE: Turn off the radio!

MARY: Why? Is it annoyin' you? Try closin' the door, that always
 helps.

JOE: What're you doin' this for, Mary?

MARY: What am I doin', honey bunch? I thought you wanted me
 to be happy.
 [*Sound of baby wailing.*]

MARY: Oh, go an' see what's the matter with Mikey, will you
 sweets?

[JOE *rushes across and turns off the radio.*]

JOE: You tryin' to make a fool of me, is that it?

MARY: Why should I want to do that? You're such an expert yourself.

[*He raises his hand to strike her. She grabs his wrists.*]

PAT: Joe!

[*Pause.*]

MARY: If you ever touch me again, I'll kill you. [*Pause.*] Give me the car keys.

JOE: What are you gonna do?

MARY: I'm going for a drive, is that all right?

JOE: You'll have a smash.

MARY: That'd simplify things, wouldn't it.

[*Pause. He gives her the keys.*]

JOE: What about the kids?

MARY: You look after them for once. They're yours as much as mine.

[*Pause.*]

JOE: When'll you be back?

MARY: I don't know.

Scene 14

As in scene 12. In addition, the sound of water dribbling into a stainless steel basin.

Pause. TONY *enters. He is about* DAN'S *age, perhaps a little older. He has a slightly pudgy face, perhaps a moustache. He is dressed casually.*

TONY: Oh, Dan — I'm glad you're still here.

DAN: About bloody time. I was beginning to think you'd forgotten me. How are you?

[*They shake hands.* TONY *notices* MIKEY *asleep in the armchair.*]

DAN: My brother.

TONY: Have you enlisted him to the cause, comrade?

[DAN *laughs. Pause.*]

No, I hadn't forgotten you.

DAN: Well, what's the story?

TONY: Did you hear the news?

DAN: No. What?

TONY: Someone tried to assassinate Joyce.

DAN: Didn't get him, ay?

TONY: No.

DAN: That was bad luck.

TONY: It was very suspicious.

DAN: They arrest anyone?

TONY: Yes, they got three people a couple of hours ago.

DAN: Who?

TONY: I didn't know any of them. Students or something. The police claimed they were party members.

DAN: Like last time, ay. What's that do to the grand scheme?

TONY: It raises certain difficulties.

DAN: I bet it fucking does.

[*Pause.*]

TONY: I take it you know why we wanted to see you?

DAN: Look Tony, you know what I think. The Labor Party'll stab us in the back as soon as it suits them.

TONY: The executive doesn't think so.

DAN: Well fuck 'em. They haven't worked with the cunts. Fuckin' trade union bureaucrats and reformist cretins. Anyone worth a pinch of shit is already in gaol. The rest aren't even worth picking up.

TONY: What you don't seem to understand, Dan, is that we are in a very similar position. A united front is our only choice.

DAN: A united front with fucking what? Dickheads who think the bosses are gonna hand over the keys because they've made a goddam awful mess of the whole fucking thing? Jesus Christ, Tony, where's the fucking analysis in that?

[*Pause.*]

TONY: There are no other options. Either we press for elections or we do nothing.

DAN: Why not join up with the other pinkos and fight it out?

TONY: Most of them are dead, Dan. [*Pause.*] The party was never geared for revolutionary violence. You know that as well as anybody.

DAN: It's a bit fucking late to realize that, isn't it?

TONY: Better late than never.

DAN: What about Lunn and all the others? What's gonna happen to them?

TONY: As soon as the elections are announced we can begin agitating for their release.

DAN: They'll be dead by then.

TONY: Well, what do you want us to do? Jeopardize our chances in some mad heroic gesture? The coup took us by surprise, don't you understand? The party has practically been decimated. We could hardly organize a football match at the moment.

[*Pause.*]

DAN: So it's been decided?

TONY: Yes.

DAN: What about me?

TONY: You won't reconsider?

DAN: How the fuck can I? You're wrong, Tony, and they're gonna kill you. One day you'll be looking down the barrel of a gun with the cunt on the other end saying "Thanks for the ride, buddy." We've got comrades dying in the streets. The least you could do is start a dialogue with the guerillas.

TONY: Gris was betrayed by an anarchist, did you know that?

DAN: Who said?

TONY: The police announced —

DAN: Since when have you started believing the police?

TONY: It was confirmed by the POM.

[*Pause.*]

DAN: This anarchist, was he tortured?

TONY: No. It was his idea of a joke or something.

[*Pause.*]

DAN: Jesus Christ.

TONY: He was executed by the authorities on Monday. Pablo Ibbietta.

DAN: Ibbietta? But he and Gris were friends. [*Pause.*] What sort of fucking world are we living in?

[*Pause.*]

TONY: It's been decided that it would be better for you to go into exile. We can arrange everything through the British Embassy. [*Pause.*] You're a romantic, Dan. At the moment we need realists. [*Pause.*] When can you be ready?

[*Pause.*]

DAN: I want to see my father first.

TONY: How long will that take?

DAN: Can you get me a car?

TONY: It's not very safe out.

DAN: I asked if you could get me a car.

[*Pause.*]

TONY: Yes.
DAN: An hour then.
TONY: All right. Wait here. [*He exits.*]
    [*Blackout.*]

Scene 15

DAN *and* JOE *sitting opposite each other in armchairs.* JOE *is wearing pyjama pants. He is fifty-eight. No sound effects. Long pause at beginning.*
JOE: Why didn't you come to your mother's funeral?
    [*Pause.*]
DAN: She was dead. There was nothing I could do. [*Pause.*] How you been keepin'?
JOE: All right. Yourself?
DAN: Yeah, I been all right.
    [*Pause.*]
JOE: You on the run? [*Pause.*] I told you, didn't I. I told you again an' again. Don't get mixed up in things. Too late now. [*Pause.*] Your mother, she could never understand the way you turned out. Weren't the way you was brought up, that's for sure. We give you everything an' what'd we get back? [*Pause.*] How bad is it?
DAN: I'm leaving the country.
    [*Pause.*]
JOE: Where you goin'?
DAN: I don't know.
    [*Pause.*]
JOE: Knew it'd come to this sooner or later. Glad your mother isn't alive to see it. [*Pause.*] Why'd you do it for, Dan? Why wouldn't you listen to reason? Gettin' involved in them things. They was none of your business.
DAN: What's the matter with you? Haven't you got fucking eyes? Look at the place! They've turned it into a fucking prison.
JOE: Because the likes of you was demonstratin' an' killin' people.
DAN: Jesus Christ. [*Pause.*] You never understood, did you? What did you want me to do? Turn my back on the whole thing? You bring me up to believe in truth and charity and then you want me to ignore what's going on in the world. You can napalm fucking peasants to the shithouse and still receive communion on Sunday. The cops can murder blacks

in the streets, but the rule of law still holds. Did you ever ask whose law? Didn't you ever ask why you ate bread an' dripping an' them on the North Shore fed steak to their dogs? Fuck me dead. If you wanted me to be anything else, why didn't you just teach me how to cheat an' swindle a fortune for myself an' leave it at that.
[*Pause.*]

JOE: It doesn't do no good to fight. You just do what you can an' after that it don't matter.
[*Pause.*]

DAN: Yeah, well it's over now. [*Pause.*] Why don't you say something to me, for God's sake? Why didn't you ever say anything to me? Were you frightened of me? Don't you think I needed you?
[*Pause.*]

JOE: I could never think of anything. You kids were better educated. It was like you was livin' in a different world. You knew the names of countries I never even heard of. I felt stupid. You with all your high-falutin ideas 'bout how things should be. I couldn't understand. If we ever talked you'd twist things around so a man wouldn't know up from down. An' you'd sneer at me, like I was nothin'. I worked all me life for you kids, doin' things a man shouldn't have to do, an' did you ever thank me? Did you ever do the things I asked you? No, you just slapped us in the face. You treated us like dirt. All the time talkin' 'bout the workers. What about me? I was a worker. You wouldn't even pass the time of day with us. Trottin' off with all your university friends to talk about things you didn't know the first thing about. Oh, you knew the theories all right, but you never had to live it day in day out without no hope an' no future. You thought you was gonna change the world. Well, you made a fine mess of it, didn't you. Hurtin' an' killin' people. That's one thing you forgot, isn't it? Comin' to me talkin' about truth an' charity. We never brought you up to become a murderer.
[*Pause.*]

DAN: I always tried to do what I thought was right.
[*Pause.*]

JOE: You ever comin' back?

DAN: I don't know.
[*Pause.*]

JOE: I'll see you then.
    [*Blackout.*]

Scene 16

As in scene 14. Rain as before. DAN *is standing.* TONY *enters.*

TONY: Ah, you're back. Good. How was your father?

DAN: He was all right.

TONY: Are you ready to leave?

DAN: I want to go to Italy instead.

TONY: What?

DAN: Italy. It doesn't make any difference to you, does it?

TONY: No, no. In fact there's quite a large *émigré* community
    there. I'll give you the name of a comrade. You can work
    with the solidarity group.
    [*Pause.*]

DAN: Yeah, why the fuck not.

TONY: Right then.
    [*Pause.*]

DAN: We're fucked. You know that, don't you Tony.

TONY: Of course, but that's no reason to give up. If we gave up
    every time we were fucked we'd get nowhere.

DAN: We are nowhere.

TONY: Ah! But we haven't lost ground.

DAN: You're a lunatic.

TONY: You take things much too seriously, Dan. We're losing now,
    but ze dialectic, mine friend! Ze dialectic vill save us! No —
    really, the army is on the point of mutiny. The trade
    embargo is literally destroying the economy. Even ASIO is
    upset about being lumbered with all the political murders.
    One of the comrades, a psychiatrist, was telling me the
    other day that he has a patient who can't sleep at night
    because he tries to murder his wife — a member of ASIO. In
    a few months, maybe, the whole thing will collapse.

DAN: A few months?

TONY: Years then. The important thing is that it can't last for
    ever. It's not the end of the world, Dan. The struggle goes
    on !

DAN: You crazy bastard.

TONY: What else can you do?
    [*Blackout.*]

Scene 17

The kitchen. JOE *is sitting at the table. The sound of cars passing along the highway. It is early morning.* MARY *enters. Pause.*

MARY: Did the kids wake up?

[*Pause.*]

JOE: No. [*Pause.*] Where did you go?

MARY: I just drove around for a while.

[*Pause.*]

JOE: I'm sorry for sayin' the things I did. I had too much to drink, that's what it was.

[*Pause.*]

MARY: Why do we always have to have arguments for, Joe?

[*Pause.*]

JOE: The first ten years are always the worst, that's what they reckon, isn't it? [*Pause.*] You gonna stay.

[*Pause.*]

MARY: I've got nowhere else.

[*Pause.*]

JOE: I could get you a flat, if that's what you wanted?

MARY: No, I want to stay with you, Joe. I still love you. I'll love you no matter what you do. I'll always love you.

[*Pause.*]

JOE: I love you too.

MARY: Things'll get better. All we have to do is stay together. The storm'll blow over. It's times like these that make a marriage strong. If we just get over this bad patch, it'll be clear sailing, don't you think?

JOE: It's gonna be better. We'll make sure it is.

MARY: Oh Joe. I do love you. Let's do things together like we used to. We could go to the beach for your birthday. You'd like that, wouldn't you?

JOE: Yeah.

MARY: We've got to do things with the kids. These are the most precious years, when they're little. The time goes so quick. They'll be men before we know it. If we enjoy what we've got, it'd be enough to fill up a lifetime. Even if we don't have any money, we can still be happy, can't we Joe?

JOE: Yeah. Yeah, it's gonna come good again. We've taken each other too much for granted, that's what it was. But now it's gonna change, I can just feel it.

[*Blackout.*]

Scene 18

This is the scene from which the play is named. It is JOE'S *birthday.* JOE *dressed in bathing trunks and carrying a plastic bucket. He is looking blankly across the water.*
The sound of surf. Children playing.
MARY [*off*]: Come on, love. Have a piece of birthday cake.
    [*Blackout.*]
    [*The sound of the surf increases in volume.*]

END

Irish Stew
John Bradley

To Elizabeth

Ron May (Captain), Greg Silverman (Allan), Tony Brown (Ian), and Garry Cook (Rae) in a scene from the La Boite premiere of *Irish Stew*.

Irish Stew was first performed at La Boite Theatre, Brisbane, on
2 February 1979, with the following cast:

IAN	Tony Brown
RAE	Garry Cook
ALLAN	Gregory Silverman
CAPTAIN	Ron May
CREW	Brad Collett
	Jeremy Head
TRIXIE	Kathleen Mahony
MAN	Chip de Deurwaerder

Directed by Sean Mee.

DESCRIPTION OF CHARACTERS

IAN
RAE
ALLAN — Three male characters dressed the same in grey drab suits. They are late middle age. Their speech is for the most part of the play slow and their actions poorly coordinated.

CAPTAIN — Smartly dressed, well spoken, English to all apparent observations.

CREW — All dressed in normal sailors' garb. Irish accents.

TRIXY/ WOMAN — Plays two roles. Dressed cheaply. Talks smugly. Appears worldly compared with others. Heavily made up.

MAN/MAN — Plays two roles. Dressed drab suit.

SCENE 1

A screen at the back of the stage shows a film of a ship at sea in a great storm. This could be in sound if projected into a corner and serve as a distractor while characters move onto stage.

The setting is the deck of a ship. Foghorn sounds loud and strong. Flash up central spot, catching three men frozen with fear as if they have been caught by a searchlight. Fade out. There is the roar of the sea and the throb of engines.

Lights come up slowly to dim, revealing the three men, all about the same height, who look almost the same, and are dressed in the same manner of drab greyish suits, small caps, and big black boots. Although they appear Irish in character, and the location of the ship they are on is somewhere in the Irish Sea, this play is not about the Irish. The three men are slow in thought and seem uncoordinated, even allowing for what would be the natural rolling of the ship in rough seas. They are sitting jammed together into one seat giving the effect of crowding.

Long pause. The atmosphere of fear and tension, as people passing by — the other three thousand on board.

IAN: Well, the sea's beginning to get up again boys. Reminds me of the last time I came over ... in thirty-nine.

RAE: You've never been over here before. How could it possibly be the same? They crowd us on these English ferries like cattle ... fodder for English factories.

ALLAN: The last time you came over you never even landed. You were rejected as an undesirable alien.

RAE: Sent home because you were more than unwanted ... regarded as a threat to life and limb.

IAN: But I was going to enlist, but they didn't want me!

RAE: It was your enlistments here that worried them.

ALLAN: The press gang of O'Connell Street. [*Pause.*] At least this time we've been picked.

[*Pause.*]

RAE: I wish that noise would stop. I can hardly hear you blokes over the noise.

[*The sound of the sea seems to choke and stop, and at the same time the searchlight image returns. They look at each other.*]

[IAN *gets up.*]

Christ! I'm sorry!

IAN: I was not part of that bunch. The group of twelve or so that I led were peace loving and well directed ... men ... who merely roved around calling others to follow a cause which was Catholic and therefore just.
[*The searchlight dissolves. Sound of sea returns at low level.*]

RAE: You weren't very successful. . . .

IAN: Rubbish. I finished up with thousands following me.

ALLAN: That was just during the Saint Patrick's Day march of thirty-seven because your parish's Holy Name Society had the turn to lead.

IAN: Well ... I had thousands following if only for a fleeting moment. And it's the numbers that count, not the reasons for numbers. Our war has always been a war seated in religion! Don't forget that, Rae!
[RAE *jolts to life.*]

RAE: What war? What are you talking about?

IAN: Come on now, try to keep up. I'm not a television set. You've got to think a bit when you're dealing with me.

ALLAN: Let's be honest with each other, Ian. Even though it might have begun as a religious war, we've been left alone now for some time to practise as we please. . . . to assemble when we like ... to say what we like . . . . We no longer want this country to be freed of religious persecutors. We want it for ourselves ... Ian, Rae, and Allan, the three revolutionary musketeers standing together for ourselves.
[IAN *becomes very agitated. Goes to grab* ALLAN.]

IAN: I ought — I ought to kill you for that, you prick. . . . You've lost sight of the cause ... the real ambition of the movement. You're the one who's let us down. By losing sight of the cause you've made us lose the respect of the people . . . . There are those who still remember O'Connell Street ... Easter Sunday ... persecution after years of service to an empire we built.
[*Pause.*]

RAE: There are precious few left who remember. This generation likes the idea of three score years and ten. They do not want to endanger their lives in war ... much rather die on the highway through their own choice than be shot up some dark alley because of someone else. [*Pause.*] It doesn't make sense to us older ones, but it seems important to them to go on ... living.

[*Pause.*]

ALLAN [*churlishly*]: Nobody wants to listen to our cause. The only donations we get are from people over fifty. [*Pause.*] Which is why we're reduced to this.

IAN: To what?

ALLAN: To sitting here.

RAE: Plotting.

ALLAN: To thuggery.

RAE: To blackmail.

ALLAN: To eliciting money through fear.

RAE: To getting respect through fear.

ALLAN: God-like fear.

RAE: Impotency.

ALLAN: Back to sitting.

RAE: Back to plotting.

IAN [*with exaggerated vehemence*]: Shut up the two of you . . . two puny little bastards both worried about nothing but yourselves. Look at you sitting in the corner of a crowded ferry cringing. Drawing attention to yourselves by the fear emanating from your quaking body. [*Pause.*] Don't tell me it's the wind ripping over the bow that's tearing at your flesh and making you shiver. [*Pause. Quicker.*] You only really have to spend an hour before action. Provided you can keep awake, the rest of the time should be easy . . . an inside job.

[*He sits down. They are jammed together.*]

RAE: Thank the lord you're our leader.

IAN: I am not. There is no leader. We are fused together as one massive fighting unit.

[*Silence.*]

[*Slowly the roar of the sea comes up. They are forced to shout.*]

ALLAN: God, if only the wind would drop.

[*Again the sounds of the sea seem to choke and the searchlight image returns.*]

[*Silence.*]

IAN: Sit, Rae! And shut up!

[*The searchlight dissolves again. Sea noises up.*]

We might have found the most secluded spot on the ship, but still we're hardly out of earshot or the line of vision. [*Pause.*] Now calm down, both of you. Things will be all

right. We've never had it so good. There must be three
thousand souls on this ferry. Three thousand potential
hostages all crammed together under one roof. Never has
there been the possibility for such a massive hijacking. If we
pull it off, they will have to meet our demands. The
authorities will have to release all prisoners and give us the
money to refurbish our armoury.

[*Pause.*]

[RAE *and* ALLAN *move forward as if having a vision.*]

RAE: You're right, of course. Now I see it all.

ALLAN: Once we get all our men out of jail we'll be back to full
strength and be able to induce fear by force.

RAE: Thousands will come to touch our garments . . . to hear us
speak.

[*Pause.*]

ALLAN: The money and the numbers, that's all we need . . .
making sure we give a little to the Church, of course, and a
little here and there throughout the country. [*Pause.*] The
giving of money is the best propaganda. What people will
do for just the smallest amount of money!

IAN: Now listen carefully. You can forget morals and principles
and consider only money. [*Pause.*] People cannot see,
hear, or taste principles, so although they may talk about
them and pretend to adhere to them, it's money and power
they care for.

[ALLAN *grabs him. He is confused.*]

ALLAN: Hang on! That contravenes all you said before.

RAE: Yes, that doesn't make sense. You said seated in religion.

[*Pause.*]

IAN: Tell them it's a cause seated in religion . . . in morals and
principles. [*Pause.*] Make sure they realize money and
power make the world tick. Show them the connection with
morals and principles — for example, through Church and
state. All they need is inference to be convinced.

[*They touch one another.*]

ALLAN: The recruits'll come rushing in.

RAE: We'll be the leaders.

IAN: There'll be more than twelve this time. I'll achieve
something this time. Sticking together over all these years is
going to finally pay off. [*Pause.*] We'll have many more
followers than before . . . thousands . . . a new order . . . a

new freer religion. [*Pause.*] That is ... more money and power.

[ALLAN *sits down.* RAE *pats* IAN *on the back, pretends to bow to him.*]

RAE: O mighty leader.

IAN: What's up with you, Allan? What are you moping about now? [*Pause.*] Always at the point of ecstasy you destroy our optimism by sitting there with a long face ... the epitome of despondency. [*Pause.*] I should've killed you years ago when I had the chance. But no, I hung on to you ... protected you ... fed you ... nurtured you, until I loved you. [*Pause.*] Now I couldn't get rid of you if I tried. [*Pause.*] How quickly you make me feel like you.
[*Silence.*]
[*He shuffles about.* RAE *looks helpless and pats both on the shoulder.* ALLAN *looks up.*]
We're locked in this together to the bitter end. No matter how bitter it might taste. It would be the end of us. [*Pause.*] This is the only action we've ever thought strongly enough about to complete.

ALLAN: I have to be sure, that's all. I have to be sure before I make this move, that's all. [*Pause.*] I haven't made many right moves in my life. Correction ... I haven't made any right moves in my life and I want this last one to be absolutely perfect ... no hitches. We must be sure of every step ... no calculated risks. That's been the trouble up to date. Always at the last minute I've panicked and rushed ... always the same end disappointment.
[*Pause. The focus drops.*]
I don't want us to make the same mistakes as that other hijacker.
[*Pause.* IAN *and* RAE *turn on him.*]

RAE: Which hijacker? What do you mean by trying to scare us half to death? Painting black images ... digging deeply into hidden recesses ... repressed corners of my mind ... things put aside because they're too horrible to think of. You know how easily frightened I am.

IAN: Yes, you little shit ... you bloody little poofter bastard ... you pile of ....
[*He stops and turns* ALLAN *round. Goes to strike.*]
Whenever I'm nervous the violence of my father works its way to the top and my baser nature takes over. [*Drops his*

hand and smiles.] The kindness of my brother wins out.... Go on get your joke over. I'm sorry. I'm just nervous, that's all.

[ALLAN *looks downcast.*]

ALLAN: It's no joke ... it's for real.

[*He acts it out, getting caught up in his own description.*] This hijacker, nationality unknown ... cause unknown ... destination unknown ... had stowed away in a jumbo jet. The biggest air-hijack in history... it would've been. Imagine ... imagine him leaping out of his hide ... gun pointed tensely... firmly held in two whitening hands ... knuckles of one clenched round black butt... knuckles of other supporting ... fastened to wrist, steadying for impact. Recoil. Fierce look in the eyes, flashing ... carefully distorted with violence. Sucking air.

RAE: What ... what happened to him?

IAN: Shut up, Allan! I don't want to know. Whatever it was it serves him right.

ALLAN: When it got airborne he leaped out of the loo only to be confronted by tons of frozen meat carcasses. [*Pause.*] It was an air transporter. [*Pause.*] Well you may laugh ... but imagine ... for days he's avoided detection ... how heart-broken, after months of planning, to find yourself on the wrong plane confronted by frozen meat ... locked in the frozen meat compartment for thousands of miles, facing nothing but corpses ... all of his fervour destroyed by one mistake.

IAN: I wonder what he said to them.... Take me to your butcher .... The inflationary impact would cripple a small country. [*Pause.*] What did happen to him?

ALLAN: The navigator heard scraping and banging against the huge sealed door behind the cockpit area and looked through the glass window at a blue cadaverous figure pointing a gun and seemingly screaming.

RAE: Did they succumb to his wishes?

ALLAN: No! They just turned up the refrigeration and left him there.

[*Pause. They stare at each other.*]

IAN: I suppose they came back occasionally to laugh at his shivering form, I'll bet.

[*Pause.*]

ALLAN: Yes! I guess we can all laugh at someone experiencing the agony of living — suppressed. [*Pause.*] He probably had a cause as just as ours. He believed in it. He was willing to die for it. Of course it probably was contrary to the normal stream of society, but that didn't make him a criminal . . . only different.

IAN: Hey! You don't have to convince us. Come over here. You don't want to create a bad impression. I've already told you about keeping your voice down. With all these people jammed together above decks sitting shoulder to shoulder . . . crushed in sitting position both inside and out . . . jammed in chairs with hardly an inch to spare . . . old ladies, old men, pregnant women, and children jockeying for positions on the stairs, trying to catch a bit of sleep. [*Pause.*] You talk about the frozen carcasses. What about this lot?

[*Pause.*]

[ALLAN *moves across to sit down. They crush together. They light cigarettes in the wind — a difficult task.*]

How was he killed? By freezing to death?

ALLAN: No. He wasn't so lucky. He was still alive when he arrived. They invited him to give himself up . . . move away from the plane. They had to unload the meat. [*Pause.*] But how could he? He was so cold his weapon was frozen to his hand. [*Pause.*] As he came out they waited till he was clear of the plane. Apparently they only had inexperienced marksmen that day. They thought he went for this gun . . . yes, the one frozen to his hand. The first one got him in the leg . . . the second one between the legs. It took him over an hour to die. [*Pause.*] He was left screaming and writhing on the tarmac as blood oozed from his wounds. Don't touch, they all screamed, he might be fused . . . They couldn't get any sense out of him, the authorities said. [*Pause.*] Oh well! It was only a hijacker. [*Pause.*] That's what I'm worried about — the fact that they gave no quarter to a human being. If a dog had been treated like that there would have been a public outcry.

[*Pause.*]

RAE: Remember the story about the boy and the pet weasel . . . .

IAN: You mean the one where he came in . . .

ALLAN: And found the weasel eating the baby?

RAE: Yes, and he grabbed the weasel, bashed its head against a brick wall, and then threw it out the window.

IAN: The RSPCA wanted to have him sent to a boy's home.

ALLAN: What a society.

[*Pause.*]

IAN: This is it . . . . You can expect no quarter, therefore there can be no slip-ups. And there will be no slip-ups if we stick to plan. [*Pause.*] We have a captured audience, so to speak.

[*The roar of the sea.*]

[*Blackout.*]

SCENE 2

An overhead projector is brought on. On it waiting to be shone on screen is a list of statistics, given below, plus plan of the ships bridge. Also at the ready is a slide projector containing a slide of the CAPTAIN *and another of the crew (could be a humorous slide, e.g., at a Christmas party). Also a slide of an English ferry and a slide of passengers. The scene is dim. The characters still outwardly appear to be on the ship, but it has taken on the appearance of a briefing room. The roar of the wind, etc., dies.* IAN *moves towards equipment, brings it on stage.* ALLAN *and* RAE *show signs of astonishment, and approach the equipment suspiciously.*

ALLAN: What the hell's going on here? Here we are on the pitching deck of a bloody ferry for all apparent purposes appearing inconspicuous . . . in an ever-worsening weather situation with the wind already at force five, and you trot out an overhead projector. [*Pause.*] Just look round . . . look up there . . . who'd believe it . . . devices . . . . [*Pause.*] Look . . . people all crowded together sitting shoulder to shoulder on a wet deck on a cloudless night in a howling wind, and you expect them not to take notice of what you're going to be doing.

RAE: You just warned me about drawing attention to myself, and here you go bringing in these things which you are going to flash up on the bulkhead wall and expect nobody to see.

[*Pause.*]

ALLAN: Yes, why do you do it?

IAN: Because life eludes me and excludes me from the time that devours me. [*Pause.*] Did I say that?

RAE: I guess so! I heard you.

IAN: Irrelevant . . . . I've had dreams. [*Pause.*] Give me credit for being an artist . . . .

[*Pause.*]

[*He comes over and guides the other two into positions. They persist in their display of lack of coordination.*]

Let's just say that we're no longer on the ship. Let's just say that this is no longer the deck but a briefing room.

RAE: You can't just say that. It's not even possible that such ... such things ... devices ... could be found on board a ship ... ferry.

ALLAN: You just can't step in and out of time whenever you please.
[*Pause.*]

IAN: I have to be burdened with concrete minds.

ALLAN: Rubbish! My mind's as subtle as yours. I've had dreams.

IAN: Then since time is arbitrary and man-made, let's change things and make it pre-boarding time.
[*Pause.*]

RAE: But why didn't you give the final briefing before boarding time.

IAN: Because it wouldn't be as interesting or as final. [*Pause.*] Being an artist, I'm a man removed from time and hence should twist it to please. Our job is not only to hijack but to make it an interesting hijack ... a clever one. So we'll finish planning it right under their noses. [*Pause.*] Our task is to tell everybody about the hijack but not let them find out.
[*Pause.* RAE *and* ALLAN *go into a huddle. When they speak, it is very dejected, i.e., "down language".*]

ALLAN: But that's not possible.

RAE: It's insane. How can you possibly hope to fool these people?

IAN: By telling the truth ... by being detailed ... by giving them visual proof of the truth ... by talking about it at length. [*Pause.*] They'll turn off after fifteen seconds, thinking it's an educational talk on the ship.

ALLAN: Very extra ... ordinary.

RAE: Yes, you're an artist all right.
[*Pause.*]

IAN: At last it's sinking in.

ALLAN: Hang on. You're not going to get off that lightly. Come back here. [*Pause.*] You can't play those tricks on me. You said you'd be making it more interesting ... therefore these people will catch on.
[IAN *flicks on the overhead projecter with statistics.*]

IAN: What people?

[ALLAN *looks around.* RAE *checks about also. They wander
to edge of stage, etc. Silence.*]
RAE: I could've sworn.
ALLAN: A miracle.
    [IAN *laughs.*]
    [*The statistics below are shining on the wall.*]

STATISTICS OF HIJACKING

Date	Successful	Unsuccessful	Total
1930	1		1
1947	1		1
1948	6		6
1949	3		3
1950	3		3
1953	1		1
1958	3		3
1959	3		3
1960	6		6
1961	6		6
1962	1		1
1963	1		1
1964	1		1
1965	1		1
1966	3		3
1967	6		6
1968	33	5	38
1969	70	12	82
1970	46	26	72
1971	24	38	62
1972	37	33	70

IAN: I can see your interest is immediately attracted to these
    figures. I always marvel at how people are attracted to
    ordinary Arabic notation as if it had some marvellous
    Eastern aura. [*Pause.*] Such figures have already
    confirmed in your minds that things happen in threes . . .
    except in the last part where three almost goes into
    everything with a little bit left over.
ALLAN: What about three into one?
IAN: Shut up! [*Pause. Consults fingers.*] Oh yes! Goes three
    recurring.

[*Pause.*]

RAE: Yeh! That's funny, that is. I've never really believed it till now.

IAN: I'm glad of that. [*Pause.*] Now look at this . . . the first air-hijacking. Try to imagine the shock to the rest of the world when the small South American aircraft was hijacked back to South America. [*Pause.*] It took me three weeks to find that information. They must have all been appalled when the small paragraph appeared on page thirty of the *New York Times.*

[*Pause.*]

ALLAN: But can you picture it? [*Pause.*] Above the roar of aircraft engines . . . the whistling and screaming of the wind and pitching and pocketing of some ancient aircraft, a poor Peruvian peasant stands up and screams "Fly me back to Lima." . . . Such people seem only to know one way . . . down. [*Pause.*] Seven million dollars in gold aboard, and he wants to return to the cold, inhospitable Peruvian plains . . . to live only where freezing cold south-westerlies blow for ninety per cent of the year. [*Pause.*] Such figures are crushing.

RAE: How did you know the story?

ALLAN: Such stories are hidden behind simple Arabic notation.

[*Pause.*]

IAN: Well, what do you think?

ALLAN: All this has proved that hijackings have become more popular . . . more fashionable.

RAE: You've a clever mind.

ALLAN: I've had dreams.

IAN: Look here! Phenomenal, no hijackings during the war. I guess war either justifies hijackings or nullifies it by not allowing the common person time to hijack. Perhaps there is no right or wrong in war, just purposeful destructiveness. Oh, I can see how you're all interested. Look again. [*Pause.*] From here down begin the unsuccessful hijackings. Why? [*Pause.*] Why, you may ask? Hang on a minute.

RAE: The planes never left the ground.

IAN: Hey! No! No! I've got it. [*Pause.*] You see, up to here planes were being flown from left to right from Communist countries to Western democracies. [*Pause.*] That was all right. Served those fucking commies right for being born on the wrong side of the Iron Curtain. [*Pause.*] But here strange, fanatical, and insane political factions began to inconvenience the white Western traveller. [*Pause.*] That made it wrong. [*Pause.*] Cut it out! Concentrate ... this is serious political polemics. [*Pause.*] Look at the success rate of those hijackings from 1930 to 1967 — better than fifty per cent. But as we get to the top end of the information, the chances of being successful lessen. Hence sea-jacking. [*Pause.*] We're going to rejuvenate hijackings on the sea. [*Pause.*] Nobody looks at the sea any more. Here we stand a better chance.

ALLAN: No. All this has proved is that there are more causes.

RAE: More causes by minorities ... more causes by minority groups which need advertising.

[*They get carried away acting out their ideas.*]

ALLAN: It pays to advertise.

IAN: It costs to advertise.

RAE: Imagine if minority groups were allowed to advertise ... internationally ... free of charge on all television networks with no restrictions ... once a week ... at prime time.

ALLAN: Like Malebio Cigars.

RAE: That's been banned.

ALLAN: Like pet foods ... only more realistically ... no holds barred ... the stark truth in colour ... make it real pet food. [*Pause.*] Put the Pet in the Can.

RAE: There'd be no need for hijackings. The message would saturate even the most violently opposed. [*Pause.*] A hearing ... and to be heard sometimes is all that's needed. Being listened to comes later.

ALLAN: No need to threaten lives. Support would come according to merit. Millions spent in annihilating hijackers could be poured into subsidizing advertising for them.

[*Pause.*]

RAE: We'd be out of a job.

ALLAN: No we wouldn't. We'd have new roles ... whiter ones.

RAE: Executive material.

ALLAN: Smart suits ... fast cars ... women and wives. Sinning on the side of right, that's important. To be on the right side and sinning, that would be nice. [*Pause.*] It'd be as good as being a rich man telling everybody how hard life is.

[*Pause.*]

IAN: Now, having wasted five minutes, let's go back to previous time and have a look at our target.
[*Slide projector flashes up ship.*] Prime target ... English Standard Ferry, which we will hijack.
[*Next slide is blank. Something appears to be wrong.*]
[ALLAN *and* RAE *start to make shadows on screen.*]
Cut it out, you two.
[*They stop. They fidget and proceed to sleep.* IAN *is still trying to fix the caught slide.*]
Bloody machines .... Sorry for the language.
[*Slide projector flashes up slide of crowds getting into ferry.*]
Prime hostages ... well fatted crowds of tourists and locals on the way back to England following a Bank Holiday weekend ... having exploited the poor Irish bookmaker at the Limerick races. [*Pause.*] Allan, wake up ... Now give Rae a shake .... Can't you possibly concentrate on what we're doing ... just a bit longer.
[*Slide projector flashes up slide of bridge crew.*]
This lot are not to be killed. If you have to, only shoot them in the leg or something. They'll be unarmed and typically frightened, particularly when they see your specially rehearsed wild looks. Take a good look; they'll be the ones on the bridge.
[*Pause. Slide flashes up shot of* CAPTAIN.]
Hey! Wake up, you two! ... God, why does the final hour find me always alone! ... Come on, you two, the night is still young. Come on, get to your feet.
[*Pause.*]

ALLAN: Can't you leave us alone. We've been over this a thousand times or more.

IAN: It's part of the decision-making process to ponder constantly what you are about to do. Our task is not an easy one, and I would give anything to have the pressure of decision-making pass me by, but we cannot allow it to pass by no matter how ignominious the end may seem. [*Pause.*]
We've been chosen for it. [*Pause.*]
There, they've dropped off again ... so the decision will finally be mine. [*Pause.*] No it won't! I'll have no Gethsemane here.
[*He shakes them and drags them to their feet.*]

Behold the captain and man who treasures his prize and is
the one who is our treasured prize! Don't cast any blemishes
on his stark white jacket. Any blemishes will lessen his
authority and render us powerless to bargain.

[ALLAN *and* RAE *come alive suddenly.*]

ALLAN: There, I told you there were problems.

RAE: What if he doesn't co-operate?

ALLAN: Orders the destruction of his radio or something?

RAE: We'll have to torture him.

ALLAN: Force him by using skilful psychological persuasion.

RAE: Make him bleed all over his stark white suit.

ALLAN: The most modern methods will always work.

RAE: Like breaking an arm ... slowly ... backwards.

ALLAN: You win every time.

IAN: He won't bleed ... he's English. According to my grand-
mother, they don't have blood like us. It's below them to
have blood. [*Pause.*] The only blood I've ever seen spilled
is our boys'. So you see it's not blood I'm talking about. Just
don't touch him till you're sure. They bruise easily ... pale
skinned. [*Pause.*] Check your violence. Is that clear?

ALLAN and RAE: Yes, brother.

[ALLAN *comes up to him pleadingly.*]

ALLAN: But you admit the possibility of failure. I'm getting too old
to fail. [*Pause.*] This world can't stand failure. Failure is
the leprosy of the age of materialism. Nobody wants to
touch you if you're a failure. I've had many. [*Pause.*]
There are younger men waiting in the wings for their
chance ... hoping.

[RAE *joins him.*]

RAE: For us to falter .... just the slightest stumble will be enough
cue for them to come leaping out kicking us to the ground in
the scramble to get ahead. [*Pause.*] Our impetuosity has
left us. We are reflective and furtive.

IAN [*affectionate but down in his language*]: You're becoming
dangerously introspective ... just a sign of age. [*Pause.*]
Fancy pondering death at this stage. Any sacrifice will win
thousands of doubters and make converts who will work for
the cause.

RAE [*agitated*]: Nobody told us that this was the sacrifice.

ALLAN: Don't you care for yourself?

IAN: I am the cause.

ALLAN: But what about our families?

IAN: You gave them up when you took up the cause. Spare some time and there'll be no need of sacrifice.

ALLAN: I hope not. I love my body the way it is ... so alive. [*Pause.*] Slow ... but alive.
[IAN *goes to the overhead projector. Puts on drawing of ship's bridge.*]

IAN: Right, let's get back to briefing .... Here's a drawing of a typical bridge. [*Pause.*] We will enter from door on the left here. Bridge crew will be at positions here and here.
[*Pause.*]

RAE: Where'd you get this information?

IAN: Out of a book.

ALLAN: What if they didn't read the book?

IAN: Stop it!
[*Silence. It lasts some moments.* IAN *shakes himself and continues.*]
They'll not see us enter because their eyes will be fixed on the instruments. The night being as ugly as it is there'll be no need for them to have a lookout posted. [*Pause.*] The bridge will be dim ... green and blue lights flickering, lighting up the intense faces of our targets as they strain to hold the ship on course. [*Pause.*] Allan ... you'll move stealthily to this side of the bridge here. Rae ... you'll move to this point here. I'll double into the captain's sea cabin and bring him out through this back door. [*Pause.*] On the given signal ...

ALLAN: What signal?

IAN: The prearranged one.

RAE: How are you going to signal without telling them?

ALLAN: I've got a good idea. Let's synchronize watches.

RAE: That's novel. Let's.
[*They set watches.*]

IAN: Now! [*Turns back to briefing.*] Right .... on the given time signal ... we'll burst in ... all lights will come on, and I'll make the announcement ... The captain, pale and drawn over the tension of the storm and now this new trauma, will acquiesce immediately for the good of his ship and his passengers. [*Pause.*] A signal will be sent out. To the world. Our cause will be explained again in detail ... conditions outlined. With such a large group of British Nationals on board, all the world will be concerned and

involved. Our success will only be a matter of time . . .
millions and men.
[*Pause.*]

RAE: What if we get in there and they're waiting for us?

ALLAN: Lurking behind half-latched doors clutching machine
pistols lovingly . . . feeling all that power . . . like the young
boy before killing his first bird . . . rubbing their hands over
cold metal, flicking safety catches on and off . . . hoping that
we will come soon, so they can dispatch us and get back to
their tasks.
[*Pause.*]

RAE: You see, you have no answer to that . . . . I don't want to go
bursting into a room where doors are spotlighted, where
like the actor on the stage I become the sole source of
somebody's amusement for a few minutes . . . getting my
belly shot out by armed critics . . . looking down watching
pieces of my flesh fly, through dimming eyes . . . hearing the
crash of bullets all round bulkheads through failing ears.
This would provide little amusement for me. [*Pause.*] Lots
of laughs for others, yes . . . but at this stage of life I've
grown fond of me.
[*Pause.*]

ALLAN: And it's not the kind of act I like to follow. There aren't
any encores after an act like that. [*Pause.*] How can you
dismiss those suspicisons?
[*Pause.*]

IAN: It's nice to see you so active before the real show . . . . How
can I dismiss them? Have you told anybody? . . . Well and
good. How could they possibly know we're here? [*Pause.*]
Now lie down and rest while I ponder the final details.
Write out our message to the world again . . . ridding it of
imperfections. Careful punctuation and spelling impress
businessmen no end . . . and completely fool politicians.
[*Silence.*]
[*They sit down. The overhead projector and slide projector
remain on for a few moments.* IAN *turns them off.*]
[*Blackout.*]

SCENE 3

*The stage is set up as the bridge of a ship. It is in total darkness.
Comes up to dimness. The sound of the sea is now roaring.*

Further effects could be added, e.g., film of ship in storm. The three are stumbling and falling over each other. The bridge crew are on stage and their shadows can be seen wandering about. The three men hold onto one another, pitching back and forth. IAN *carries a small briefcase. All have small hand guns.*

ALLAN: It's getting real bad out here now. We're going to be forced inside soon.

IAN: What about the plan?

ALLAN: To hell with the plan. Let's get out of this.

RAE: Keep your voice down. That bloke might be still following us.

　　[IAN *turns and stumbles back.*]

IAN: What bloke?

RAE: I've never known a blacker night . . . the devil's night. Let's get it over fast.

ALLAN: I can see a light up ahead.

IAN: That must be the bridge. It's usually located about here . . . facing the front.

　　[RAE *kneels.*]

RAE: Shouldn't we pray first to make sure God's still on our side? [*Pause.*] When we go in there we may have to kill or even be killed.

　　[*There is a shudder from one of them. They kneel and pray silently. They jump up.*]

ALLAN: Like my mother always said, get God on side and then you'll be right. I never found out how you could be sure, because the other side also prayed to him I'm told. [*Pause.*] All wars are in some way in the name of religion. [*Pause.*] Who's first in?

　　[*They are suddenly thrown across stage. Sometimes they end up on top of one another. They are pitched back.*]

IAN: I think you should go first, Allan.

　　[*They are thrown about.*]

ALLAN: But you've always been our leader.

　　[*They are thrown about.*]

RAE: I would, but I've always been the quiet type . . . afraid to show my hand . . . unable to make the liaison between human and human which is so necessary in being a leader.

　　[*They are thrown about.*]

IAN: I was never made leader by choice or design. You've always just assumed that I'm your leader.

　　[*Pause. They are pitched about.*]

RAE: Therefore you should go in first. There is nobody as well co-ordinated as you, who can open the door.

[*They are pitched about.*]

ALLAN: We've got to get off this deck . . . before we're killed.

RAE: We're drawing too much attention. I feel a crowd gathering.

IAN: Where?

[*With a seemingly almighty plunge the ship throws them into the bridge. Immediately all lights come on. The bridge is in complete disarray. Crew members are drinking and singing. Nobody is tending the instruments. Nobody notices the new soaked and suited messes on the floor. They lie there for a while. Party-goers step over them laughing, etc., taking no notice. The three get up and pass among the party-goers.* THE CAPTAIN *appears rolling drunk with woman.*]

IAN: Silence!

[*Nobody takes any notice.*]

RAE [*shrilly*]: Hey, you there, shut up!

ALLAN [*shouting*]: Haven't you any respect for authority!

[*Nobody takes any notice. They drop their hands, look disappointed.*]

IAN: It's always the same; nobody notices us. We wouldn't be here if people had ever listened to us. If we want to get anywhere we'll have to use force.

ALLAN: Violence.

RAE: Unmitigating threats.

[*Pause. Still the din goes on. They wander around the room hopelessly disoriented, shaking and pushing people who treat them like any other party-goer until they meet back at the first point.*]

RAE: I want a pee.

ALLAN: I want a bog.

IAN: I want to be sick. [*Pause.*] Where can we go?

[*Pause.*]

[IAN *jiggles with his wet clothes. His revolver falls to the floor. There is absolute silence.* IAN *picks it up. The other two point weapons menacingly. The crew wander back to their places.* THE CAPTAIN *takes his place behind crewman on wheel.*]

IAN: Hell, I forgot about those . . . Instant control . . . not a word spoken . . . . Go on, out, the rest of you; we don't want you yet.

[*Pause.*]
[*The party-goers leave. The crew take up assembly positions.* THE CAPTAIN *orders them to positions, scaring the life out of the Irishmen-hijackers, who run helter skelter in confusion. Finally:*]

RAE: We've won.

IAN: I did it.

ALLAN: Yeah!

IAN: Oh, if only my mother could see me now . . . her dreams . . . for me . . .

ALLAN: If only all our mothers could be here . . . stable outgoing sons . . . achieving ambitions.
    [*They begin to walk to what seem to be set positions but bump into one another.*]

RAE: Fancy worrying about whether or not we were going to be able to get on with people or not. [*Pause.*] Look how marvellous we're all getting on now.

IAN: Who'd want to be a priest after all the converts we'll have after this show.

ALLAN: Yes, my early love for the life of a religious has just been surpassed by the admiration I'm now being given.

RAE: Benediction after benediction. [*Pause.*] They look as if they would be only too glad to give up everything and follow us.
    [IAN *laughs.*]

ALLAN: Even their wives.

IAN: That's right, the bitches.
    [*Pause.*]

RAE: Said I had a little dick and laughed. Every time she pointed and laughed. I didn't even get to use it.

IAN: Said mine was too thin.

ALLAN: Said mine was too thick.
    [*Pause.*]

RAE: Penis envy. The harlot got every man round to get into her bed.

ALLAN: They were always hanging round.

IAN: Waiting for me to go out.
    [*Pause.*]

ALLAN: We're clever how we can communicate. Everybody else seems mute.
    [*Pause.*]

IAN: Should never have left home.

RAE: My father threw me out.

ALLAN: The bastard was always drinking... coming home drunk... smashing up the place... and my mother.
[*Pause.*]

IAN: She loved me so.

ALLAN: I used to sleep with her.

RAE: Snuggle in together in the depths of winter in a far corner of the room... protected... while the old man would go about smashing and cursing all of us.

ALLAN: Finally dying in a heap of vomit on the bathroom floor.

RAE: But not before he kicked me out.

IAN: Writhing in agony she was... as he raped her in front of me. [*Pause.*] I should never have left her. She needed me to hold her up... a goddess... shimmering through the darkness amid chaos.
[THE CAPTAIN *confronts them as if it's the first time he has seen them. He still speaks drunkenly but retains balance. Hijackers not so; they are constantly thrown about during speeches.*]

CAPTAIN: What do you mean by trying to take this ship by force? When there's a party going on. You could've knocked.
[*Pause.*]

RAE: What's he talking about?

ALLAN: I don't know. He's English, isn't he?
[*Pause.*]

IAN: I went to England, but I didn't talk to anybody and nobody talked to me. Always busy. I seem to be familiar with his dialect, though. [*Pause.*] I wonder how he found out.

CAPTAIN: Come on, get on with it. We're busy people on this bridge, as you well can see. [*Pause.*] Will you stop rolling about. One of the guns will go off.

IAN: Well, stop the ship rolling.
[*The gun in his hand moves about menacingly.* THE CAPTAIN *waves his hand. The ship now stops rolling (seemingly). The three hijackers nevertheless remain basically unco-ordinated, e.g., they trip over unseen objects.*]

CAPTAIN: There you are. I've brought the ship about. Is that all you want?
[*The three men slowly take up position.*]
Well, come on, talk... don't just stand there. What do you want now?

ALLAN: You talk to him Ian. Surely he'll understand you.

CAPTAIN: Will you stop this bloody babbling, you bastards.

[RAE *moves to him quickly.*]

RAE: Don't you swear at us. I recognize that kind of language. Don't you use filthy language when I'm around . . . you filthy man . . . you dirty . . .

ALLAN: We'll kill you for that. I think I'll blow your skull off right now for that. You don't deserve to live after using language like that. An obscene hole, right here . . . to match the obscenities . . .

IAN: I agree, but don't kill him yet. It would be suicide to kill him . . . suicide. All would be lost again.

[*Pause.* THE CAPTAIN *is slowly released.*]

CAPTAIN: You're hijackers . . . and you're going to hijack this ship.

IAN: That's right. We're hijacking this ship.

CAPTAIN: An act of piracy on the high seas punishable by death. [*Pause.*] No wonder you act so harshly . . . pushing people round.

[ALLAN *shoves somebody with his gun.*]

RAE: You said it, Captain. We're tough and dangerous. [*He hits* THE CAPTAIN *across the mouth.*] And I hate people who use bad language. There's no need for filthy language. It clearly shows a man with bad morals . . . just like my father. . . a moral cripple. [*He hits him again.* THE CAPTAIN *falls.*] They don't bleed, you know.

CREW: Stop it! You'll be kicking next.

[IAN *turns and kicks a crew member.* RAE *kicks* THE CAPTAIN. *The crew member doubles over on floor.*]

IAN: Anybody else want to argue? . . . Don't try to use violence on us or we'll retaliate so hard you'll wish you were dead. It's not just a rumour we're tough.

CAPTAIN: OK. Where do you want to take the ship to?

[*The three look at each other.*]

ALLAN [*aside to others*]: We hadn't counted on that question. What'll we do?

IAN [*aside*]: This man's no idiot. We'll have to play it by ear. [*Pause.*] [*To* CAPTAIN] To sea. Where else would you suggest that hijackers take a ship?

CAPTAIN: Somewhere away from this storm.

[*Pause.*]

RAE: Get this boat the hell out of this storm and quick.

CAPTAIN: Away from the coast?

ALLAN: Away from the coast. Where else do you find the sea?

CAPTAIN: There's no need to threaten me. I'll do as I'm told. I've everybody on board to think of.

[ALLAN *comes at him with his gun.*]

RAE: Yes, you think of us. We're very important to you now. We're going to make your name famous. You'll be the captain of the first hijacked ferry. Remembered in history books. *Guinness Book of Records.* Immortalized in song ... like some ancient mariner.

IAN [*stopping him*]: You've got it wrong. We're the ones who will be immortalized.

[*Pause.*]

CAPTAIN: What do you want to do now?

ALLAN: Don't talk to me. I don't want to say. It's not really my position to say. I am more a man of action. Words always fail me.

[*Pause.*]

CAPTAIN: I suppose you'll want to communicate something via radio. [*Shows them the radio room. Pause.* ALLAN *shoves him.*]

IAN: Don't order us about. Just tell us where the radio room is and we'll leave you alone.

[RAE *shoves one of the crew.*]

RAE: Don't be frightened. I'll only kill you if I'm forced to.

[*Pause. Everybody is still and silent.*]

CAPTAIN: Well! What am I to say?

ALLAN: Where?

CAPTAIN: On the bloody radio.

ALLAN: Don't get smart. We've warned you about that filthy language.

[THE CAPTAIN *gets a backhander. Struggles to his feet.*]

CAPTAIN: I guess I'll report we've been hijacked.

[*Pause.*]

IAN: Yes, you report that. That's your job.

[*He opens a small briefcase, rustles through papers, finds the right one, and hands it over.*]

And here's a list of instructions we have for you to broadcast to the world and everybody on board. [*Pause.*] Now read them for us.

[THE CAPTAIN *begins to read slowly and objectively. He reads the whole message blandly with no recognition or emotion.* IAN *mouths the words intently as it is read.*]

CAPTAIN: Now hear this ...

RAE: That's original.

CAPTAIN: This is the captain of the English Standard Ferry out of Dublin. I've been instructed to read the following statement by a group who have hijacked this vessel.

[*Pause. Hijackers draw themselves up.*]

You are now all hostages on board this ship. As foreigners of all nations other than ours, you're therefore being used to forward our political and economic ends. [*Pause.*] We are loyalists, minority loyalists who for centuries have been ignored and have been nothing but the chattels of a great Western power who has bled our country dry for her own selfish ends. [*Pause.*] We have been ignored. [*Pause.*] Because we are a small group without any money we are ignored while powerful and rich lobbyists gain more power and more money. [*Pause.*] We have carried out this action firstly to be listened to. Our plea is to be left alone to work out our own destiny whatever it might be. We loyalists will guide the people of our nation towards that destiny in whatever way we see fit. [*Pause.*] All of our fellow loyalists — guerillas to you — who are presently locked away for their belief must be released and sent home immediately, no matter what their crime. They must be granted safe conduct. [*Pause.*] Four million pounds must be deposited in a Swiss account. [*Pause.*] Failing this, the ship will be sunk with all hands. Nobody will be spared. Long live the cause! [*Pause.*] This statement is the view of a militant organization describing itself as loyalist and in no way represents the view of the master of this vessel or the company who owns it.

[*Pause.* THE CAPTAIN *stands open-mouthed. The men are congratulating each other.*]

It's a very expensive radio message.

IAN: Couldn't have done better myself! Put in all the right pauses. Intonation magnificent.

RAE: Pity we're all so shy.

ALLAN: Reticent.

[*Pause.*]

CAPTAIN: It's unreal. In no way is it seated in reality. Its terms are preposterous. Who would care whether this ship would sink or not?

[*The three move in on him.*]

ALLAN: What do you mean?

RAE: What are you trying to imply?

IAN: We've done everything right so far, haven't we?

CAPTAIN: You haven't done anything except fantasize!

ALLAN [*grabbing* THE CAPTAIN]: You're going to be filthy again.

IAN [*jumping in and separating them*]: Don't grab him like that.
You'll crush his uniform and he'll be judged as unfit to lead
men.
[*Pause.* THE CAPTAIN *regains composure.*]
Now tell us what you mean by everything being unreal. Is
that meant as a criticism?

CAPTAIN: Certainly not .... Well ... it could be if you wouldn't
hurt us.
[RAE *shoves a crew member. Lines his pistol up on
another's head.*]

RAE: We haven't touched you and we won't if you tell the truth.

CAPTAIN: Well, it's just that ...

ALLAN: This better be pleasant. I'm sick of all this down talk.

CAPTAIN: There are no British nationals on board this ship.
[*Pause.*]

IAN: You liar.

RAE: Trying to distort the truth.

ALLAN: This was planned down to the last detail.

IAN: We waited for the August Bank Holiday ...

RAE: To make sure that the boat ...

ALLAN: Would be crowded with aliens.

CAPTAIN: You've been given the wrong information. [*Pause.*]
Can't you just take my word for it that the ship is occupied
only by Irish. [*Pause.*] Since the trouble began, the
authorities have kept all the real aliens away from the
ethnics. Saves them from getting the wrong impression.
[*Pause.*] You have literally missed the boat.

IAN: You're crazy. This boat is filled with English aliens. It says
so on this piece of paper, and each one of us has a piece,
making three to one.
[*Pause.*]

CAPTAIN: Probably a triplicate copy. See, even you have your own
bureaucracy ... probably layers of it.
[*Pause.* ALLAN *hits him.*]

ALLAN: Using words with sexual overtones again. All you can ever
use are words dealing with things below the belt ...
fleshpots ... filth ... filth. [*Pause.*] You ought to know by

now how filth stirs me up. [*Pause.*] Like all the really good
people, I can see it . . . I can see it.

CAPTAIN [*dragging himself up*]: You can ask anybody here.

RAE: We're going to ask everybody here.

ALLAN: You don't need to tell us what to do. Everyone is going to
have to prove where he comes from by who he is.

CAPTAIN: It'll take a lifetime.

ALLAN: Don't interrupt . . . Well, we'd better hurry up.

[*The Irishmen huddle close together.*]

IAN: It's all becoming clearer now. I see it all as if I'd been here
before. The memory of being held down . . . almost . . . as if
by a huge hand.

ALLAN: Pressing me in the chest . . . flattening me against the
floor . . . trying to take away life's breath by forcing its way
through skin and bone.

RAE: Then gradual release . . . and the feeling of the stiffness in
the bones . . . like the left impression of the handshake of a
long gone friend . . . and wanting to extend fingers and toes
till they drop off.

IAN: Pushing . . . pushing . . . slowly rising . . . becoming lighter
and lighter till the feeling of water surrounds me and I am
floating like the ship, rocking . . . rocking.

ALLAN: I raise myself up out of myself . . . and walk around.

RAE: I can see it now.

IAN: The gaining of control, always it has been in my vision. The
admiration of a deed . . . finally . . . well done.

ALLAN: Don't say any more.

[THE CAPTAIN *signals crew to take up assembly positions.*]

RAE: I don't want to go back to the time before this event. It's all
been perfect so far.

[*They suddenly realize the crew are standing before
them.*]

IAN: What's going on?

CAPTAIN: The crew members are lined up for interrogation.

IAN: Shouldn't they be looking after the ship?

CAPTAIN: You asked to question them to see whether or not they
were Irish.

[*The hijackers move aside and stand in a circle.*]

ALLAN: Who's going to take on this job?

[*They look at each other.*]

IAN [*to* ALLAN]: I thought you would. You're the most
provocative.

RAE [*to* ALLAN]: You've always been the one to put foward ideas. You must have the questions.

ALLAN: I'm not going to ask men personal questions about their heritage. [*Pause.*] I'm too easily embarrassed.

CAPTAIN [*comes across*]: Why don't you ask them if they're Irish?

[*They stand there mute.*]

Come on! They can't stand around all night. They've got jobs to do. Ask them: Are you Irish?

[RAE *gives him a shove. He staggers back into the wheel and breaks it.*]

Look what you've done now! A million-to-one chance... years of constant steering. It was well worn but...

RAE: It's all your fault. You bumped into it.

ALLAN: What'll happen now?

CAPTAIN: We'll start to circle. All direction will be gone.

ALLAN: Don't you carry a spare?

CAPTAIN: Why?

RAE: Serves him right. He shouldn't interfere.

CAPTAIN: Don't you realize ...?

RAE: Are you Irish?

THREE CREW MEMBERS [*together*]: Yes.

CAPTAIN: You're lucky the storm is beginning to abate, so that we can circle without much roll.

RAE: Is he still on about it?

[*Pause.*]

ALLAN: It's interesting, Rae.

[*Pause.*]

CAPTAIN: While it is circling it will continue the path travelled until eventually we will just spin on one spot.

ALLAN: That'll be confusing.

[*Pause.*]

CAPTAIN: Maybe I should stop all engines.

IAN: You're not taking over here. You're not going to stop anything while we're going somewhere. [*Pause.*] How do we know you're not lying?

[*Pause.*]

CAPTAIN: Look at the compass.

RAE: Don't tell us what to do. I like the view from where I am.

[ALLAN *goes over to the ship's compass and smashes it.*]

ALLAN: Now nobody knows where we're going, so you can all

assume we're going in a straight line. You see, we're not real dumb.

CAPTAIN: Oh shit!

[RAE *turns on him and hits him. He falls to the ground. The hijackers speak aside.*]

RAE: Well, what now?

ALLAN: More questions, I guess.

RAE: I've had my turn.

IAN [*to* THE CAPTAIN]: Come on, get to your feet, man.

CAPTAIN: God . . . I . . .

[RAE *smashes him to the ground again. He is spreadeagled.*]

RAE: Don't you try any of your anti-religious views here, boy. I once belonged to holy orders, and although I might have been asked to leave, at least I tried to get closer to God. I just didn't fully realize he wasn't of this world.

[THE CAPTAIN *remains out.*]

ALLAN: You might have really hurt him that time, Rae.

RAE: A price he should be willing to pay for being a leader.

IAN: But if he is damaged beyond repair, then all will be lost. There'll be mad panic once it is known the head has been cut off. Remember the chicken in the fowl run with no head at Christmas? It would run anywhere, spilling blood senselessly.

RAE: He's all right. I'll try not to hit him again. But he asks for it. You heard him. [*Pause.*] He directly provokes me.

[THE CAPTAIN *is lifted into a chair. He is supported. They mill around like seconds in a boxer's corner. Gradually he comes round.*]

CAPTAIN: How do I feel?

[*Pause.*]

IAN: How do you feel?

CAPTAIN: Wrecked . . . like my ship!

IAN: Then you'll have to stop provoking my colleagues and me.

CAPTAIN: Yes, I realize that. If only I could find out what it was that was so provoking in what I said.

RAE: Try accent.

ALLAN: You were helping us with our inquiries into the Irishness of these crew members.

CAPTAIN: Don't use force on them.

RAE: Only if we have to.

CAPTAIN: They'll tell the truth.

ALLAN: We'll recognize it.

[*Pause.*]

IAN: Now that's settled, let's get on with it.

CAPTAIN: What about your fathers?

IAN: Describe your fathers.

[*The three crew members speak together in a slow manner. If this proves too difficult, they should each speak certain sections. They must give the sense of unity. They speak with accent despite the formal English. They read automatically, as if reciting from navy manual.*]

CREW MEMBERS: My father was a heavy drinker . . . always on the bottle. [*Pause.*] He wasn't a dumb man . . . just a very sensitive one who after years of being hurt took to the bottle . . . no, bottles. [*Pause.*] It was only after many years of frustration that he took to beating me and my mother . . . and the rest. [*Pause.*] Finally there was nothing left. He gave up. [*Pause.*] My mother's prayers were answered. [*Pause.*] How she prayed!

[RAE *silences them with a hand. Nevertheless the three hijackers show they are moved.*]

RAE: You'd better be telling the truth!

CAPTAIN: What greater proof that they are Irish. [*Pause.*] Continue and describe your mother.

[*Pause.*]

ALLAN: We'll ask the questions here. [*Pause.*] What are your mothers like?

[*Pause.*]

CREW MEMBERS: Oh, she's still as lovely as ever . . . always on her knees praying for father and me. Father's the bad one. [*Pause.*] The devil never possessed so much of man. [*Pause.*] When he'd come home drunk she'd just drop to her knees in front of him and pray all the while as he beat her. [*Pause.*] Then for hours after she'd lie there groaning and praying to God as the children would be trying to help her broken body stay together. [*Pause.*] How she would clasp us all round her . . . just like the Holy mother and like Jesus suffering with the little children.

[*The hijackers wander about bewildered, looking at one another.*]

IAN: I don't know, it sounds so much like my mother. They must be . . .

RAE: Yes, but . . .

ALLAN: We need more . . . more words. We must be absolutely sure before . . . . The accents could be put on. Their clothes aren't Irish.

[*Pause.* THE CAPTAIN *comes up to them. The hijackers seem to be cringing.*]

CAPTAIN: Anything else?

RAE: They haven't said anything about themselves.

CAPTAIN: What about your own personal lives?

RAE: How dare you ask them a personal question? We're in command here . . . . Ask them.

CAPTAIN: I did.

CREW MEMBERS: I was born alone . . . but unlike other members of my race . . . I stayed alone. [*Pause.*] Always hovering in the background . . . never speaking till forced to. [*Pause.*] At school I would stand in the shadows of stairwells while everybody passed by . . . catching glimpses. [*Pause.*] I would wander for days among the other lads without a word passing. A dreamer, they said I was. [*Pause.*] I was, I guess. [*Pause.*] Dreaming of boats and ships and the floating feeling. [*Pause.*] I suffered the terrible feeling of having something large down my throat and being unable to do anything about it.

[*Pause.*]

CAPTAIN: But surely there were girls?

[RAE *leaps across but trips and falls.*]

RAE: You're being filthy again. Luckily for you I tripped, otherwise it might have meant the end.

[*Pause. During the following speech the hijackers become more and more agitated.*]

CREW MEMBERS: There were never any girls. Some would come up to me and stand in front impish like . . . smiling . . . rubbing their tongues over their teeth. [*Pause.*] Talking sweetly . . . hands on hips and letting them slowly wander down their thighs to the bottoms of their skirts, playing with their skirts till I ran away. [*Pause.*] No matter how hard I tried to reach out and touch their smooth soft skin or soft hair . . . something held me back. [*Pause.*] Nobody talked to me. Nobody touched me. I was sterile at the most potent time of life. [*Pause.*] It was then I knew I had a vocation. I was chosen by God, that's why I was different. [*Pause.*] I was stranger than others. I could resist temptations that came from being close to people. [*Pause.*] I could be constantly assaulted by the flesh and resist —

ALLAN: Stop! You've said enough. You men are innocent.

RAE: You're Irish. You've suffered . . . been forced into corners.

IAN: I can't listen. You must be exhausted. Go back to your positions.

CREW MEMBERS: But there's nothing to do. Everything is destroyed. The ship is slowly going round and round in its own whirlpool.
[*Pause.*]

CAPTAIN: Stand by your posts. We will at least be seen to be orderly if this thing spreads.
[*Pause.*]

ALLAN: Leave them alone. Can't you see they've had enough of your orders. You've turned them into robots.

IAN: It's a wonder with their backgrounds they haven't ended up hijackers like us.

RAE: Yes, I wonder why not?

CREW MEMBERS: Our dreams are constantly being fulfilled by being at sea all the time.
[*The hijackers huddle together in a group.*]

IAN: What are we to do now?

RAE: Who have we left is probably more to the point.

ALLAN: I wish it would come to an end. There's no point in dragging it out when the probable outcome will be as always.

IAN: Don't talk about it. [*Turns to* CAPTAIN] Well, come on, you've had all the ideas up to now, surely you must have some more.
[*Pause.*]

CAPTAIN: I don't know. I've just begun to realize my Irishness.

RAE: You liar! You'll pay for your sin of being born elsewhere.
[RAE *goes again to hit him, misses, and smashes some instruments.* RAE *writhes in pain.*]

ALLAN: How can you be, with that high-class accent?

IAN: An Irishman in charge of an English ferry?

CAPTAIN: An Irish ferry, you mean. Half the ferries that ply the trade are Irish. I received all my education in England, sure, but I'm only one generation out of step. I've lived in England, sure, but that doesn't make me —

ALLAN [*grabbing him and twisting his arm*]: You're lying! Tell the truth before us and God.

CAPTAIN: God . . . Yes, ask me if I'm a Catholic. Go on.

IAN: Are you a Catholic?

CAPTAIN [*in pain*]: Funny you should ask that question. Yes.

RAE: Don't let him get smart. I'll fix him with a good right cross.
[RAE *swings punch.* THE CAPTAIN *ducks.* RAE *punches* IAN, *who is close.* IAN *doubles over, whimpers.*]

ALLAN: Look what you've done now.

CAPTAIN: You've damaged your leader.

RAE: We have no leader.
[*They slowly bring* IAN *round. During the process, their awkwardness is further highlighted. Their movements, to be accurate, have to be slow and deliberate.* IAN *comes round. They put him on the floor.* THE CAPTAIN *watches. The crew maintain their positions.*]

IAN: What's happened? Rae, you'd better sit down. It's always the same when you get worked up. You always miss by miles.
[*The three sit down and merely stare ahead. They begin to rock back and forth slowly.* THE CAPTAIN *comes up to them. Puts his hand on each.*]

CAPTAIN: You haven't finished with me yet.

RAE: We haven't finished with you yet.

CAPTAIN: But it's no good having me as a hostage. I am supposed to always sacrifice myself for my ship.

ALLAN: Not if you're an Irish captain.
[*Pause.*]

CAPTAIN: It makes no difference once at sea. It's only you individuals who have a nationality. They'll sacrifice me just as an example to all other captains. They don't care how individuals think and feel, which is why you're here.
[*Pause.*]

IAN: There must have been a reply on the radio by now, surely.
[THE CAPTAIN *goes over to the radio-operator. He takes off phones.*]

CAPTAIN: They want to know if there's been a reply.

RADIO OPERATOR: The airwaves are very heavy at the moment. Signalled for a reply and sent a Mayday, but nothing back.

RAE: How can we believe you? How can we trust anybody? You, captain, may have been the person constantly watching us . . . shadowing our every move, waiting your opportunity to confuse us with sophisticated machinery like this.

CAPTAIN: Go on. Touch that machine. It won't bite.
[RAE *shoves it off the table.*]

I didn't mean that. I was being physically facetious.

RAE: Well, that'll teach you to toy with us.

CAPTAIN: Now you've ruined everything. We're now being held incommunicado, like a college of cardinals. [*Pause.*] I've never known three people so bent on self-destruction.

IAN: You've never known enough people.

RAE: It's for a good cause.

[*Pause.*]

CAPTAIN: Now to contact us they'll have to first locate us and then negotiate person to person.

ALLAN: A good point. Once they listen to us face to face they won't be able to deny our demands.

CAPTAIN: Can't you face the reality that they are going to blow us out of the water?

IAN: They can't. We're Irish.

CAPTAIN: Because we're Irish.

RAE: There are innocent aliens on this boat.

CAPTAIN: All the better, you and your organization will be blamed.

ALLAN: Look around. We're surrounded by holy men. God will not allow three thousand dedicated followers to be destroyed.

CAPTAIN: God needs such followers with him.

[*Pause. The Irishmen huddle like children.*]

IAN: We'll find somebody on this boat.

RAE: Somewhere.

ALLAN: Tie him or them up to the mainmast.

IAN: We'll question every . . .

RAE: Passenger . . .

ALLAN: Until someone cracks . . .

IAN: And tells the truth.

[*Pause.*]

RAE: Then we'll have a hostage.

[*As the conversation finishes, the three are huddled together in centre stage.* THE CAPTAIN *is seated. The crew stand by their ruined post. Silence.*]

SCENE 4

Setting lights gradually come up. Everything is smashed and in disarray. There are no controls that seem to be working. THE

CAPTAIN *is sitting but only with great control. The hijackers are sitting huddled.*

RAE: How many do you think we'll have to interview?

ALLAN: About three thousand, he said.

CAPTAIN: You'll never get through them.

RAE: Yes we will. We'll group them according to families. What is true for one must be true for all.

CAPTAIN: God, I think I'm going to be sick.

ALLAN: Why don't we send out a questionnaire? After all, it would be to the advantage of most of them. [*Pause.*] Being in all probability a suspicious-looking lot, it would save them from subsequent torture.

IAN: Some could fill out the questionnaire twice... helping friends whose honesty would preclude the hiding of their true identity. [*Pause.*] I think the personal touch is needed.

ALLAN: So do I.

RAE: I do too.

IAN: Then it's agreed. We too will become hardened in our determined search for the truth.

CAPTAIN: Pure fantasy. It's all in the mind.

IAN: I didn't hear that. It could go very hard for you if you begin to insult us as before. [*Pause.*] Remember... I see from your colour you do.

RAE: Yes, we have little need of you, the direction we're heading.

CAPTAIN: Where are they going to follow you to? [*Pause.*] Round and round the ship... like this. [*Pause.*] Go on, you lead now. I'll follow. We'll make a great crowd. [*Pause.*] Heading for the promised forecastle.

ALLAN: Don't mock us. Don't poke fun. Can't you see we've had that kind of attitude from people like you who are always looking for the faults within people.

RAE: Come on, let's get him now.

[*There ensues a chase, during which* THE CAPTAIN'S *complete disorientation enables him to avoid the hijackers.* ALLAN *goes to shoot him.*]

IAN: No don't, not yet. We still need him and while he's spinning about like that we know we've got him.

RAE: But shouldn't we be able to control him and everything.

IAN: Our orders weren't to control, just to capture.

ALLAN: I don't feel we've done that. Look about you, things don't look right.

RAE: We didn't do that.

ALLAN: I know, but it was done when we were here, and surely that is enough.

[*Pause.*]

IAN: We weren't in control when things happened. He was.

CAPTAIN: Yes. I take full responsibility.

RAE: Yes, you're to blame all right, and after we have finished and got what we want ... then I'm going to let your superiors know of your complete failure.

[*Pause.*]

CAPTAIN: Thank God I know I won't live to see it.

[*Pause.*]

IAN: What do you mean? You're just trying to give the whole thing the kiss of death.

ALLAN: Yes, so keep your mouth shut. I dearly look forward to the opportunity of having you catch bullets between the teeth.

RAE: We only need one person who's not one of us and we're there.

IAN: Even so, they wouldn't hurt us. The growing awareness of man's past inhumanities ensures that they won't harm a whole boatload of humans.

[*Pause.*]

CAPTAIN [*holding on, steadying himself*]: Who is aware of man's past inhumanities? [*Pause.*] The average man in the street who goes on to become your average idiot politician. [*Pause.*] He can't even comprehend the word humanity. [*Pause.*] You will be destroyed. You were sent to be destroyed.

RAE: We're not frightened to die.

[*Pause.*]

IAN: I for one would welcome it.

ALLAN: We mustn't talk like this again.

RAE: I can feel a darkness settling round me ... that is wet.

IAN: Filling my eyes ... ears ... and nose.

[*Pause.*]

[*Silence, followed by a commotion. A man and a woman seem to spin through the door. They are dressed in poor clothing. The woman is pregnant. The man appears both drunk and sick.*]

CAPTAIN: Here are your first interviewees.

RAE: In the calm of the night you're suffering morning sickness.

Come on, woman, cheer up. After all, those who don't have kids reckon ninety per cent of it is psychological.

ALLAN: Must be the first, you look so perfect. A madonna worth knowing.

IAN: What's your name?

TRIXY: Some men call me Trixy.

RAE: Come on, it must be your first. Tell us.

TRIXY: Probably the first of many. Worse bloody luck.

ALLAN: Let me have a feel.

TRIXY: No bloody way. You get in line. He's first.

[*Pause.* ALLAN *tries to get round her. She has no part of it. She cannot believe what she's seeing.*]

ALLAN: Come on. My mother, God rest her pure soul, would always let me feel the babies in her tummy. [*Pause. He goes to touch her tummy and gets clip on the ear.*]

IAN: One by one they came.

[*Pause.*]

TRIXY: That's what happened all right and look at me now. [*Pause.*] Told me the more juice I got, the less chance I took. [*Pause.*] The grass never grows where the crowd treads, they reckoned. [*Pause.*] Good Catholic joke, I guess.

[*Pause.*]

RAE: I used to love the way it turned and squirmed . . . throbbing away. Come on, just a touch.

TRIXY: Go on, just a touch, but it'll cost you . . .

[*They all line up.*]

I should've checked whether this mob had the cash.

ALLAN: Good . . .

[*Pause. They each have a feel of her pregnancy.*]

TRIXY: You've got a funny sense of direction. But if that's all you want, go for your life. [*Pause. Aside to man*] I could handle this standing on my head — Hey, you brute — they're angels. [*Pause.*] Some of you men lust after your mothers all your lives. [*Pause.*] Sick, you all are, and weak . . . so weak you couldn't shoot piss-holes in the snow . . . or even leave a bloody mark.

[*The hijackers are oblivious to her words.*]

IAN: What are you hoping for? [*He smiles up into her face.*]

TRIXY: I was hoping to bloody abort. They all reckon it's easier to have the little bastard. [*Pause.*] Don't take the pill, all the men told me. It'd be a sin. No wonder all the little redheads running round all look alike. It's all those women and men who refuse to sin by taking contraceptives. [*Pause.*] So righteous. [*Pause.*] Despite all the kids face down in that cesspool they call a canal. They haven't sinned. [*Pause.*] God's justice. They deserve it... a fitting end for all bastards.

[*Pause.*]

RAE [*lovingly stroking her*]: All you women have a marvellous sense of responsibility, thank God. Where would we be without you mothers?

TRIXY: What a tough mob you are!

IAN: What are you doing on this ship? [*Pause.*] I mean, in your condition, shouldn't you be home getting ready for the happy day?

TRIXY: Have you ever attended one of those days? My God, no wonder I suffer from morning sickness. It's knowing the dream world you bloody men live in. [*Pause.*] International Women's Year to you meant one big root.

ALLAN: Shouldn't your husband be looking after you better? You'll smash into something in a minute and damage yourself.

[*Pause.*]

RAE: Yes. Your husband should get you a chair. [*Pause.*] I don't want you hurt at this point in time. [*Pause.*] That's how I lost my mother. He came in. She was pushed... heaving, panting, crying out... pushing... sweating through it all, only to die the minute the child was born. [*Pause.*] Even her final act ensured that life would continue. [*Pause.*] I was twelve and on my own after she'd left. For months I wouldn't — no, couldn't — speak. [*Pause.*] Everybody came to look at me. [*Pause.*] Only when finally alone could I really utter...

IAN: You... husband... sit her down.

MAN: I'm not her husband.

RAE: What do you mean?

[*They literally fall on him. They inflict all sorts of violence. Finally, exhausted, they give up.*]

ALLAN: Fancy denying her at this point of time.

IAN: You were seen with her.

MAN: I didn't even know her name till you asked her.

[RAE *knocks him down. Again* THE MAN *struggles up.*]

RAE: You lying mongrel. Are you Irish?

MAN: Yes.

[THE MAN *falls down before he is hit.*]

MAN: I must be dreaming.

TRIXY: Lay off him. He's not my husband. He happened to be just passing.

[*Pause.*]

ALLAN: Well, where is your husband?

TRIXY: I haven't got one.

RAE: You mean somebody did that to you and then just walked off. [*Pause.*] How could they?

TRIXY: Surely I don't have to show you?

[*Pause.*]

IAN: No. I couldn't do that to a pretty girl like you. You're something to be cherished.

RAE: To be pampered.

ALLAN: Admired, not shattered.

[*Pause.*]

IAN: Too many men see women only as . . .

RAE: Sex objects.

ALLAN: Vessels for occasional usage. How are you paying your way?

TRIXY: I'm working my passage across.

IAN: You mean you're a member of the crew.

TRIXY: Yes, many of the crew think I'm their member.

[*Pause.*]

ALLAN: What a marvellous sense of independence you show. [*Pause.*] Do you like it?

TRIXY: What else can a young girl do . . . best?

[*Pause.*]

RAE: Just you tell me his name. I'll fix him.

TRIXY: You mean them . . . a battalion of names with shadowy faces and hollow promises.

ALLAN: You mean there was more than one.

TRIXY: Yes, except for once. One brief time for a week I thought I'd made the break . . .

ALLAN [*suddenly worked up*]: Don't go on. I've seen the sweaty, smelly, beer-filled bodies standing there in dark alleyways, waiting their opportunity. [*Pause.*] My mother walking home with me from the movies. The leering laughter down an even darker street. The sudden feeling of a coarse hand on my shoulder shoving me away. [*Pause.*] Her scream muted by an even rougher hand across her mouth as she felt them upon her ... straddling her as if she were a bitch in heat. One after another while I struggled and kicked ... finally knocked out. [*Pause.*] My father always wanted to know what she had done to torment them. He refused to have anything to do with her. [*Pause.*] I never let go of her hand after that ... until recently. [*Pause.*] I had to ... you're the first person.

TRIXY: You men have a fine sense of the dramatic, that's for sure.
[*Pause.*]

IAN: What do you do that enables you to work your passage?

TRIXY: Anything, boy blue. I'll even fantasize for you. That's why they call me Trixy.
[*Pause.*]

RAE: Oh!

IAN: What'll you do when the baby comes?

TRIXY: Move into a room with somebody.

IAN: No, anything but that. [*Pause.*] I was brought up in a room with ten others and my mother, and . .. father ... never let her alone. [*Pause.*] Every night he'd be at her. Didn't worry about us kids. Didn't think we'd ever remember when we grew up ... he reckoned. [*Pause.*] Like a good wife she never knocked him back. [*Pause.*] His massive frame heaving and panting away ... throwing bedclothes every which way while twenty eyes looked on in wonderment and terror. [*Pause.*] He towered over our frail and sensitive mother, whose mission in life seemed only to gratify his emission.
[*Pause.*]

TRIXY: Nicely put ... almost poetic.

RAE: Spoken like a true Irishwoman.

IAN: You may go.

RAE: Take that thing that calls himself an Irishman with you.
[*Pause.*] Tell him to be honest when he comes to his senses.
[*They leave.*]

IAN: Remember, we are not jackals employed by big business but individuals whose dreams correspond to a cause. We are only wrong to those who think they're right.
[*Pause. They look around.*]
Where are the next two?
[*Pause.*]

CAPTAIN: Don't worry. There'll be more.
   [*The same two as before stagger in. They spin round the room.*]
IAN: I thought we were going to interview another pair.
RAE: Yes, come on you two, out you go.
IAN: Send in another two.
MAN: But we are another two.
IAN: You couldn't be. Look, you wear the same clothes . . . have the same accent . . .
RAE: Everything the same.
MAN: Have you ever left the country before?
WOMAN: Well, no wonder. We all look the same from outside. You know . . . old trick Chinese, Japanese, et cetera.
MAN: That's how you can tell that the other two thousand nine hundred and ninety-eight are all Irish.
ALLAN: How's that?
WOMAN: They all look alike.
   [*The three hijackers become threatening.*]
RAE: You're playing games.
ALLAN: You've forgotten what we're really capable of . . .
IAN: When aroused.
   [*Pause.*]
MAN: Its' the truth, man.
   [*Pause.*]
WOMAN: Of course it's the truth, man. Would a woman in my state lie to you?
   [*Pause.*]
IAN: And the baby, I guess, is not yours?
MAN: No, of course not. I was just passing by and this lovely lady asked me to step inside with her.
   [*Pause.*]
ALLAN: And do you know who fathered the child?
WOMAN: These days, who knows anything? In an age of promiscuity, who would think to tell me anything about sex?
   [ALLAN *draws his revolver. He turns round to her and points the revolver directly at her. She is numb.*]
ALLAN: Come on, woman, you must feel most threatened. There must be somebody out there. [*Pause.*] You're all the same . . . fucking liars, all of you . . . absolute pricks whose main ambition is to lead us men on . . .just filthy little turns of teasers.

[*Pause.*]

IAN: No, Allan. Don't get worked up.

ALLAN: I've had these jumped-up poofter bastards. Their eyes are hollow like death.

RAE: Allan, the language, please.

ALLAN: Oh, shut up! I must do something to square off for the years of fun-making they've had at my expense.

[*He blazes away point-blank at the woman. His shots are wild.* THE CAPTAIN *is screaming at him. The other hijackers leap at him.* THE WOMAN *has been hit.*]

ALLAN: Now can you see that though seemingly farcical and comic characters, we mean business. [*Pause.*] That hostages can be killed . . . unwillingly. [*Pause.*] Why not just stand still a second and listen to all the cries in the wilderness. [*Pause.*] Try to decipher the gnashing teeth.

[*Silence.*]

IAN: What irony! Even if it had been born, it'd be a stateless little bastard. [*Pause.*] Even if it was originally English, it's of no use to us now. Everything we touch . . . pointless except through violence . . . and even then . . .

[*Silence.*]

[*Blackout.*]

SCENE 5

Lights come up. Stage appears bathed in early morning light. All characters except hijackers seem asleep. The chaos caused by the night is everywhere. The dead woman lies draped in a chair. The hijackers are staring exhausted. When they move and talk, they are uncoordinated and slow in speech.

IAN: It's cool and refreshing.

RAE: It's good that I can still feel the day.

ALLAN: It's even better that we've stopped moving. [*Pause.*] Have you noticed how everything is normal?

[*Pause.* IAN *wanders to the edge of the stage.*]

IAN: Yes, we are becalmed like the spider in the web. [*Pause.*] Every string around us vibrating while we sit perfectly still, ignoring the singing air.

[*Pause.*]

ALLAN: We should wake them before it all passes. Nobody should miss a morning like this.

IAN: It seems a pity to disturb them. The calm seems to have penetrated deep among them. [*Pause.*] But wake them anyhow, Rae. We've got a lot of business to attend to.
[RAE *goes round kicking them. He has little effect on any except* THE CAPTAIN. RAE *brushes* THE WOMAN. *She falls out of the chair. He apologizes and puts her back.*]

RAE: I'm sorry. I forgot she was dead. She's best left undisturbed now we've had the party.

CAPTAIN [*raising himself*]: Oh my God! I'd forgotten what we had the party for, but now seeing her reminds me of the wake. [*Pause.*] Not that anything's forgiven, mind you, but at least something has come out of this incident... the feeling a man has for a woman and child. [*Pause.*] I've never seen so many sympathetic bodies at a wake before. This woman has linked us all through a common motherhood.

IAN: It's because of that fact we've decided to surrender and have you communicate through the normal channels with the authorities that we are prepared to surrender regardless of consequence. [*He goes to hand over his weapon.*]

CAPTAIN [*laughs*]: What, write them a letter of apology? That won't make any difference now, you fools.

RAE: Don't get cheeky, captain. We don't want an instant replay of last night. We haven't handed over everything yet.
[IAN *assumes stance of control.*]

ALLAN: What do you mean, it won't make any difference? Come on, spit it out. We can face the truth. I'll ...
[*He lurches towards* THE CAPTAIN, *who casually avoids him.*]

CAPTAIN: Well, if you'll all stay a minute and listen. [*Pause.*] You destroyed our compasses and wheel so that now we won't know where we are. We will also be difficult to find. [*Pause.*] Remember the Norwegian tanker. [*Pause.*] No ... like all the world you've already forgotten. [*Pause.*] An island ... for all we know it may still be wallowing around out there.

ALLAN: But it must have sunk. Every day they searched set areas.

CAPTAIN: And every night the tanker moved ... into an area already searched. The longer we remain becalmed, the more difficult it will be to find us.

IAN: Surely there must be some other way to steer the ship.

CAPTAIN: Not that I know of, or that anybody on board is capable
of fixing.
[*Pause.*]
RAE: Well, we'll just radio them up.
CAPTAIN: Oh yes! On that radio lying there. Do you think you'll be
able to put it together in time ... before we all die of old
age. [*Pause.*] We can't even tell them where we are, let
alone make changes to what was originally communicated.
ALLAN: Right oh! Cut it out. What are you trying to get at?
RAE: Trying to tell ...
IAN: Stop beating round the bush. Give us the truth.
[*Pause.*]
CAPTAIN: It is impossible for us to do anything. We will be
destroyed. [*Pause.*] Governments have become tired of
hijackers and hijackings, and it is now easier to destroy all
involved. It saves a great deal of trauma and gives the
hijackers what they really want ... self-destruction.
IAN: Lies. I can't believe that anybody would destroy a ferry with
three thousand people on it. [*Pause.*] It's whimsical, and
no government can act whimsically.
CAPTAIN: Oh, this won't be done whimsically. It will be carefully
planned by the government to discredit you. So you might
as well lay down your weapons and we'll take to the boats.
[IAN *goes to follow suggestion.*]
ALLAN: No, don't. It's a trick.
RAE: But what else can we do?
[*They look about.*]
ALLAN: Sink the ship ourselves.
CAPTAIN: But don't you understand, it won't make any difference.
It'll be reported the same.
IAN: Rubbish! If we sink the ship with everybody on board before
anybody finds us, they won't know where we are and they'll
continue looking. [*Pause.*] Never will they be game enough
to fabricate what has happened in case someone pops up
and tells the truth. [*Pause.*] There's bound to be someone.
[THE CAPTAIN *stands with mouth agape. The hijackers
appear pleased with themselves. Lights are dim. There is a
distant roar of jets. On screen is movies of jets going
through formation rolls, etc. Perhaps distance shot of
vapour trails.*]
CAPTAIN: So you at least agree that now it is inevitable that we
will be destroyed.

[*There is a sudden roar of jets. Noise level should be close to 130 dB. Movie shows low pass. The force pushes everyone to deck. The noise passes quickly — diminishes. Movie shows jets once more up high.*]
Well, let's get back to the party. We haven't much time left. [ALLAN *pushes him back to the centre of the bridge and makes him assume a position of authority.*]

ALLAN: No you don't. Give the order to pull the plug. You're still the authority here.

CAPTAIN [*laughs*]: Plug? What plug? Do you think you're in an empty bathtub and are now going to let the water in? [*Pause.*] True to the last, you remain egocentrics. [RAE *stumbles up to him and gives him a shove.*]

RAE: Don't try to be funny. You know what plugs we mean — the ones in the bottom of the ship. [*Jets roar past. Noise same as before. Film shows low pass. Noise diminishes, film shows distance of jets.*]

IAN: Hurry up. We haven't much time.

CAPTAIN: If you mean sea-cocks, I wouldn't know where they were or even if this ship had any. [*Pause.*] We're not at war so why should I ever worry about scuttling a ship?

RAE: Well, we are at war. Don't you realize that yet? We are fighting for what we truly believe is right. Doesn't that make us just as right? [*Roar of jets and film, as before.*]

IAN: Come on, where are they? You'll force us to kill you.

CAPTAIN: Oh, I'll talk . . . since it's inevitable anyhow. [*Pause.*] They're in the bottom of the ship.

RAE: Oh! Good.

ALLAN: Well, off you go and undo them.

CAPTAIN: I'm not going to do it. I don't want to be the one who loses my ship.

IAN: Well then, it has to be one of us.

RAE: You can count me out. I've got a fear of plug-holes. Ever since I was a kid and they used to warn me if I stayed in the bath I'd get sucked down the plug-hole and the firemen would have to come and get me out. I believed them then. [*Pause.*] And I still do.

ALLAN: Well, that leaves me . . . and I'm not doing it on my own. [*Pause.*] Going down there into the bowels of the ship. [*Pause.*] At the rate the water will come in, I'd never stand a chance.

IAN: You're not supposed to stand a chance anyway.

CAPTAIN: What about the people . . . the passengers? Surely they deserve a chance.

IAN: Leave them on the decks waving at the jets. They're happy doing that. They think the jets are being friendly. [*Pause.*] Let them die deluded . . . the way they've lived. That way they'll die happy.

[*Movie shows jets strafing and rocket-assaulting ship. Noise is deafening. Explosions and smoke on deck. One by one, without a sound, the crew drop down. Above it all the hijackers are shouting.*]

RAE: There you are, I told you they'd beat us to it.

[*Pause.*]

ALLAN: They're going to sink us without giving us a chance to prove ourselves worthy of committing suicide.

IAN: Come on, let's get out of this.

[*The hijackers grab lifejackets and simulate jumping into water. Silence. Their faces are highlighted. They are blackened with oil, etc. The three are holding hands.*]

RAE [*to* IAN]: It's you who got us into this mess. Look what you've achieved . . . no ship . . . no hostages . . . no freedom . . . no ransom . . . another great achievement. I think we were set up.

[*Pause.*]

IAN: I'm not your leader. I'm not responsible. I didn't apply for this job.

[*Time elapses in silence.*]

RAE: [*beginning to flounder*]: I can't hold on much longer. You're a mongrel, Ian . . . both of you are. [*Pause.*] Here are the three of us . . . common bloody thieves . . . about to die after a lifetime of failures . . . alongside those about to die after a lifetime of success.

[*Pause.*]

ALLAN: Don't despair. Hang on. This is not the time to despair. There's still a lot to be done. [*Pause.*] Even in the middle of the ocean. [*Pause.*] He's gone.

[RAE *falls down gently.*]

IAN: Well, he didn't last long. So much for all the help I ever gave him.

[*Silence.*]

ALLAN [*takes off his life-jacket and offers it to* IAN]: I want you to have this.

[*Pause.*]

IAN: Why?

ALLAN: Because you're the one who should survive. You're the best of us at talking. [*Pause.*] Maybe you can convince them.

IAN: What a beautiful gesture... two chances at survival. [*Pause.*] I'll remember you for this when they find me and take me up out of the water.

[ALLAN *collapses.*]

Now it's me the sole survivor... the only one of three thousand to make it. [*Pause.*] They're sure to come for me. Despite all their powers to devastate, they're sure there must be someone left.

[*Blackout.*]

END

The Playwrights

STEVE J. SPEARS

Steve Spears was born in Adelaide on 22 January 1951. He studied law at Adelaide University, where he became involved in university revues, both as an actor and writer. He finally dropped out of law to pursue writing as a career. His first major work, *Stud* (a musical), was performed in Adelaide in 1973. Next came *Africa — A Savage Musical,* which played to full houses in Melbourne at the Pram Factory in January 1974.

The Resuscitation of the Little Prince Who Couldn't Laugh as Performed by Young Mo at the Height of the Great Depression of 1929, or more simply *Young Mo,* premiered in The Space at the Adelaide Festival Centre. A new production by Richard Wherrett opened at the Nimrod Theatre Upstairs in January 1977 starring Garry McDonald (Norman Gunston) as Mo and Gloria Dawn as Queenie Paul.

Spears has also written for ABC radio and television programmes and has appeared as an actor in most of the Crawford series and in plays as diverse as *Dimboola, Pandora's Cross,* and *White Horse Inn.*

His best known play, *The Elocution of Benjamin Franklin,* starring Gordon Chater, opened initially at the Nimrod Downstairs and then transferred to the New Arts Theatre, Glebe, under the banner of the Nimrod Theatre and Eric Dare, where it ran for 163 performances. *The Elocution of Benjamin Franklin* had an outstanding critical success, toured most of the Australian capitals, and has been produced in the West End of London, San Francisco, and off-Broadway.

King Richard was workshopped at the 1977 National Playwrights' Conference and was subsequently produced at La Boite, Brisbane.

STEVE J. SPEARS ON *KING RICHARD*

A great wit once said that democracy was the worst possible form of government except for all the others. Yeah, well. Maybe.

A more astute commentator once ruminated that the police police us, but who polices the police?

Politics is a serious business. I mean, the things the state can *do* to you are horrifying. They can withhold the dole, send you to gaol, conscript you, keep files on you, and stick ASIO onto you. With their economic shotgun they can blast away at everybody. If those guys get you in their sights you don't stand a chance.

Such were my thoughts late in 1975 as I watched the fall of Whitlam and the disgraceful events happening in Canberra and the elections. And they're still my thoughts.

Alfred Hitchcock once said that drama was life with the boring bits cut out.

No one in *King Richard* seems to take things very seriously. From the start, Harris baits Brown more for form's sake than any real anger. "Got ya", he says. Brown's first question to Sue is: "Have you received any orders about me?" Then he rapidly starts consorting with the enemy (or, at least, a very suspicious stranger). Stuart brings important documents to Brown's room, then leaves them lying around. He even takes his "secret" prisoner to a nightclub. At the end, Dundon accepts the loss of more than a billion dollars with a rueful shrug. (A billion dollars!)

Everybody plays games. The characters in *Richard* play more than most and harder than most. And the stakes are higher than most. But they're still games.

There was a nice Elizabethan feel to *Richard* when it premièred at La Boite, as characters knock on the door, strut upon the stage and then exit to make room for another. It had that feeling of game and role-playing that is entirely appropriate to the play. We all know Richard is going to cop it in the end. We all know Sue isn't quite who she appears to be. We all know, long before the end, that Brown has switched tapes. The plot is fairly basic. True to the Chandler tradition, it is Harris — the first person we see — who strikes the mortal blow. And like all good heroes, Brown gets him in the end.

Games.

But wait, I am trying to say something. Dundon is an attractive character in his cheerful villainy. Indeed, let's face it, he is more human than the Zen-like Richard, who never seems to put a foot wrong.

Richard fights the good fight and beats Dundon, yet he does not take the next logical step and expose the premier. All Richard is concerned about is his union and the log of claims. No hero of democracy, this one.

So, while Dundon is a basic-black crook, Richard isn't pristine white. Indeed, Brown is responsible for two deaths by the end of the play, though he gets his partner in crime to execute the deed. I'm asking, then, for the audience to choose the lesser of two evils. If you empathize with Brown's need for revenge at the end, don't you condone Harris and Sue's demise? And even then you have to choose which one you feel sorrier for (as does Dundon).

Well, that's enough of that. It is tedious when the game gets too serious.

STEPHEN SEWELL

Born Sydney, 1953 — cold war — Catholic — working class. 1957 — Sputnik — space race (later, at university, I study physics and mathematics). 1961 — the Kennedy administration informs Australia that it is considering military intervention in Vietnam. 1962 — Cuban missile crisis — Australia announces that it is providing thirty military instructors "at the invitation of the Government of the Republic of Vietnam" — lies. Catholic school: communion, confirmation, confession — We live in a free country, sir. 1963 — Kennedy assassinated — my father cries as he tells me. 1964 — the Menzies government reintroduces conscription — the resistance movement begins to stir. 1966 — assassination attempt on Labor leader Calwell — Premier Askin endears himself to President Johnson by instructing his driver to "ride over the bastards" — demonstrators throw red paint at the Yankee — I hold a placard saying "All the Way with L.B.J." and take it home as a souvenir — my first demonstration, and I'm on the wrong side. I read Orwell's *1984*. 1968 — Paris on the point of revolution — the Socialist Fatherland invades Czechoslovakia — the movement against conscription begins to become a movement against capitalism. 1970 — Kent State — they're shooting at us — moratorium — victory in the air. 1971 — marriage, university. 1972 — Labor government elected —the resistance collapses. 1973 — coup in Chile — there is no peaceful road to socialism. Begin writing. 1974 — divorce and degradation. 1975 — coup in Australia — our leaders tell us to maintain our rage, but don't strike, don't take the streets, don't defend your government. Defeat. Move to Brisbane. Write *The Father We Loved on a Beach by the Sea*.

STEPHEN SEWELL ON *THE FATHER WE LOVED ON A BEACH BY THE SEA*

There may be a temptation — because of the style of the dialogue — to treat this play naturalistically — by which I mean, crudely, that where in the text I indicate "Kitchen", someone with a bureaucratic imagination will indeed re-create an exact replica of a 1959 working-class kitchen, complete with toaster and plastic rat. I might just say here that for me, theatre is actors with a space to move in, and anything that interferes with that movement — unless such restriction is part of the play — should be thrown out. Not only are props expensive and difficult to work with; they subvert the great power of theatre — the opportunity to imagine and to be surprised by illusion. Apart from this general opinion, however, I think that if you look closely at the play you will see its structure is not naturalistic — or at least provides a dimension and a dialectic that can be blunted by too literal a translation of the superficial text into performance.

The themes of the play are more or less obvious. The pre-conditions for, and nature of, working-class reaction, as well as its contradictions, and similarly those of the revolutionary Left. There is also in the play, I think, a deep sense of isolation — isolation of the worst kind — that which exhibits itself in the face of a loved one. It seems to me that by the end of the play none of the three principal characters has any substantial or meaningful relationship with the world. Nevertheless, each of them has an inarticulate hope — or at least the will to persevere.

I've got no objections to the play being labelled "political", except that it seems to imply that there are "non-political" plays, a point which I think is dubious. Is *No Sex Please — We're British* non-political? If you're unsure, perhaps you should listen a little more closely to the debates being fought by the women's movement. That this play may seem more political than what is generally seen on the stage merely indicates that the ideological content of Australian theatre is rather one-sided.

I would like to thank Alrene Sykes, Rick Billinghurst, Jeremy Ridgman, and Margaret Anne Boyle.

JOHN BRADLEY

I was born 7 August 1944. I attended various primary convents in Brisbane, completed my secondary schooling at Saint Columban's, Albion Heights, and then obtained a Diploma in Primary School Teaching; I later changed to secondary school teaching. I married in 1967, and my wife and I migrated to Canada, where I eventually became principal of a five-teacher primary school. In Canada too I continued my arts studies at the Universities of Vancouver and Victoria. We returned to Australia in 1972. I began to teach in a secondary school and completed my education degree, majoring in English and psychology.

I gave up trying to have poems and short stories published, faced with what seemed to be an incestuous medium. In 1975 I went to the Australian National Playwrights' Conference to work on what seemed to be a promising play: I have since re-written it and hidden it away. *Let Me Not Thy Vigils Keep* was my first major work, and it was workshopped at the first Queensland Playwrights' Conference. In a subsequent gruelling by fourteen actors from the Queensland Theatre Company, one of the actors suggested that since I had such a plain background I should go home and write a domestic play. I went home and wrote *Irish Stew*. I have recently completed a play called *The Asinine Man* and am currently working on another which for the moment I will call *The Take Away Family*.

I am now English subject master at Hendra State High School, and we have three children — Brendan, Stefanie, and Kate. I have always had an obsession with writing; it is in fact a constant source of distraction.

JOHN BRADLEY ON *IRISH STEW*

(John Bradley's statement is a condensation of comments made by him and by Sean Mee, the director of *Irish Stew,* in an interview lasting over an hour. The interview began with my comment that when I saw the play, I felt at first as if I were watching a dramatized Irish joke; then suddenly it wasn't a joke any more, I felt vaguely uncomfortable, the play had changed. — Ed.)

The change was deliberate. I wanted to write about some of

the absurd things I'd seen happen over the last thirty years —
Vietnam, the Palestinian guerillas being accepted by the United
Nations, this kind of thing. When I began, I thought I was
writing about the future, but events very quickly began to catch
up; the Harrisburg incident was one of them. The reality of *Irish
Stew* is not far away. People get to a point where there is nothing
they can do, they are put in a position where they are unaware of
the implications of their actions, and once they are in that
position they have no control of what is happening, just like the
three Irishmen. But you can't hit people over the head with the
kind of tragic state of where we are, because they are hit with it
every day; so you have to con them into listening, show them
something they can relate to, and then throw in the things you
want to say.

As I first conceived it, the three Irishmen were in a kind of
space where fantasy and reality were irrelevant, because both
meant the same thing. The ship's captain is the only real focus of
reality; he keeps on reminding them of the consequences of their
actions, to which they don't respond, or respond in keeping with
their fantasy, because that's all they've got. The captain is there
as a none-too-subtle reminder of what the consequences will be if
they founder; he makes the audience constantly aware that this
is a ship, this is a sea, there is a government, and there are people
on board. In the end he too is thrown out of reality.

Trixy is a fantasizer. She fulfils their need of woman as
mother and lover. Audiences react not so much to the shot but to
the horror of what is obviously going to happen to her. The whole
thing is mother based — mother images, contact.

The three Irishmen? Impotent, first. Not stupid, not even un-
intelligent — just people who don't view consequences, don't
even plan, which is apparently true of most hijackers. They plan
only the first step, the taking of the ferry, and after that they
intend to play it by ear. That's where it falls apart.

The production changed in the course of the season. Primarily,
the horror deepened. The three actors playing Ian, Rae, and
Allan had begun by playing for laughs in the early part of the
play, but as the season progressed they began to internalize and
find more and more horror in the situation. We changed the
character of Trixy; she accentuated the role of fantasizer more
and more, so that she sent up the Irishmen within the play. The
actors found this hard to handle, they were being sent up gutless;

they could take it from the captain, but not from a woman. The whole show is a metaphor for the endless rush of water, the crawling back into the womb. Once Allan shoots the woman they regress down the years.

It's an Irish joke all right, and we're all caught in it.

Other Plays Published by University of Queensland Press

Can't You Hear Me Talking to You? edited by Alrene Sykes
  Four Colour Job by Gail Graham
  Balance of Payments by Robert Lord
  Duckling by Michael Cove
  Can't You Hear Me Talking to You? by Nora Dugon
  The Boat by Jill Shearer
  Sadie and Neco by Max Richards
  They're Playing Our Song by Jennifer Compton
  Prey by Leila Blake

The Great God Mogadon and Other Plays by Barry Oakley
  Witzenhausen, Where Are You?
  The Hollow Tombola
  Buck Privates
  Eugene Flockhart's Desk (for radio)
  Scanlan
  The Great God Mogadon (for radio)